Crystal
Decoder

Crystal Decoder

Harness a
million years
of earth
energy to reveal your
lives, loves, and destiny

A QUARTO BOOK

Copyright © 2001 Quarto Inc.

First edition for the United States, its territories
and dependencies and Canada published in
2001 by Barron's Educational Series, Inc.

All inquiries should be addressed to:
Barron's Educational Series, Inc.
250 Wireless Boulevard
Hauppauge, NY 11788
http://www.barronseduc.com

Library of Congress Catalog Card No.
00-105473
International Standard Book No. 0-7641-1735-1

QUAR.CRDE

Conceived, designed and produced by
Quarto Publishing plc
The Old Brewery
6 Blundell Street
London N7 9BH

Editor Steffanie Diamond Brown
Art editor Elizabeth Healey
Copy editor Andrew Armitage
Designer James Lawrence
Photographer Rosa Rodrigo
Illustrators Kim McGillivray, Ch'en-Ling
Picture research Laurent Boubounelle
Proofreader Peter Kirkham
Indexer Dorothy Frame

Art Director Moira Clinch
Publisher Piers Spence

Manufactured by
Regent Publishing Services Ltd, Hong Kong
Printed by Leefung Asco Printers Ltd, China
Printed in China

987654321

Contents

Foreword

There are many books available on the subject of divination, yet only a small number have been written exclusively on the subject of crystals. Crystals, along with all other types of stones, have been used for healing and divination purposes since time immemorial. In ancient times, shamans and tribal healers used stones as tools for healing the sick and for divinatory work; today, alternative healers and diviners continue this age-old tradition.

Like all natural objects, crystals are magical tools which we can use to effect change and achieve harmonization. They have the power to help us along our individual paths through the maze of life by expanding our consciousness, calming our stresses, and infusing us with healing energies. Just as importantly, as natural tools, they can help us reconnect to the Earth and the universe in the midst of this technological age.

Written by an exceptionally proficient tutor and consultant, this book provides a wealth of knowledge on many aspects of the fascinating subject of crystals. In explaining some of the most important divination systems centered around crystals, and in detailing the healing powers commonly attributed to forty-five of the most powerful crystals, this book will no doubt prove an invaluable resource for those who seek to empower themselves and to improve their lives. I am sure that this book will be treasured and appreciated by both crystal novices and experts alike, whether as an introduction to the world of crystals, as a source of further insight for those already in tune to the powers of crystals, or simply as a way to enhance one's enjoyment of crystals.

Thank you, Sue, for allowing us to share in your wisdom.

Berenice Watt, president of the British Astrological and Psychic Society (1994–99)

Introduction

The mineral kingdom and the crystals it contains are the foundation of all physical matter and of life itself. Crystals themselves are the most orderly, most stable forms of matter in the entire universe. Their beauty, striking colors, and forms have always attracted attention, and yet their value goes far beyond surface appearance.

Crystals have been revered and given spiritual significance through the ages because it has been recognized that they can create profound shifts in awareness, extending normal human perceptions into the mysteries and powerful worlds of the spirits and ancestors. This quality has made crystals the focus of many different types of healing and divination techniques, from the wearing of protective amulets to casting stones to foretell the future, and from crystal-gazing to assessing and alleviating the causes of disease.

Working with crystals, whether for healing, self-development, or divination, often creates changes in how the world is seen and understood. Crystals can crystallize new patterns of mind in us. By their very nature, crystals extend beyond the human experience of time and space, making them wonderful tools to explore beyond the world we know, while their earthy origins keep us grounded in the practicalities of everyday life.

Discovering Your Potential

Crystals have been a mystery ever since the earliest peoples first found them. Their precise shapes and brilliant coloring are like nothing else on the face of the planet. In all of humankind's oldest traditions, crystals are connected to the spiritual world; particularly the heaven or sky realms, where the sun, moon, and stars dwell.

CRYSTAL KNOWLEDGE PAST AND PRESENT

There is no doubt that our ancestors were well aware of the powers of crystals. They lived surrounded by stone for thousands of years in caves, and developed sophisticated technologies using flint, a type of quartz, for all of their toolmaking. If anyone was sensitive to the energies of stone, it was our distant forebears.

The ways in which crystals, gems, and precious stones are used today is a continuation of the practice of past millennia. Throughout all this time, through changes in culture, beliefs, religions, and technology, very little has altered in our instinctive use of the mineral kingdom. Despite current scientific understanding of the origin, makeup, and useful properties of crystals, their magical hold on our imagination continues.

CRYSTAL ATTRACTION

Not everyone is drawn to explore the world of crystals, but those who feel a natural attraction to it often find that crystals can be very effective tools to help one realize one's potential.

The exploration of crystals is a process that takes the attention inward. For example, one might study the changes that occur in the emotions or thought process-

◀ *Our forebears were intimately familiar with the qualities and properties of stone. It is likely that many hours were spent shaping and polishing these fine flint axheads for ritual or ceremonial purposes.*

es of someone who touches or wears a certain crystal. Or, one might examine whether crystals cause sensations that can be felt in the physical body. Embarking on these types of investigations is bound to bring a greater awareness to the rest of the explorer's life.

ALTERATIONS OF CONSCIOUSNESS

There is no doubt that crystals alter consciousness. They can take the attention away from everyday concerns by their aesthetic qualities, like a fashionable, upmarket toy. They can change moods and emotions when worn as jewelry, or emphasize personal status and conspicuous wealth. Wearing crystals can also bring confidence to those who seek skills and virtues they believe they lack.

WEARABLE ENERGY

Because of the special qualities of crystals, they make excellent tools with which to explore the subtle realms of consciousness. For one thing, they are inherently attractive—it is easy to get lost in the close examination of a beautiful colored stone. More importantly, they can change the way we view the world by directly modifying the subtle energy patterns that make up the human body. Our forebears knew this as well: crystals were turned into gemstones, amulets, and talismans, to be worn or carried, as the energies of certain stones were thought to bring benefits to the wearer or carrier.

Perhaps for the first time in humankind's history, crystals are now widely available to large parts of the population. No longer are the magnificently expensive cut stones in jewelry-store windows the only stones for sale. In today's marketplace, gift shops, bookstores, health stores, and specialist suppliers all carry baskets of inexpensive tumbled stones, as well as beautiful mineral samples.

Sitting with a Crystal

Each time you acquire a new crystal, take time to explore how it changes your self-awareness. The more familiar you become with each stone's energy, the greater your insights relating to its uses and meanings will be.

1. *Start by settling yourself into a comfortable seat. Place the stone you wish to explore in front of you at a height from which you can gaze at it without straining your eyes.*

2. *Begin by closing your eyes, taking a couple of deep breaths, then gently turning your attention to how you are feeling.*

3. *First, tune in to your body and think about how it feels. Are there areas of tension or discomfort, or is there some other sensation?*

4. *Next, direct your attention to your emotional state and your thoughts. Are you experiencing a pervading mood? Is your mind active or quiet? Are you focusing on certain issues?*

5. *Once you have explored your own energy state, turn your attention toward the stone. To begin with, simply gaze at the crystal in front of you for a minute or two.*

6. *Close your eyes and scan your body, mind, and emotions once more, to see if you feel any differences, however slight.*

7. *Next, pick up the stone and examine it closely from all angles.*

8. *Hold the stone between your hands and close your eyes again. Note any changes that occur in the next few minutes.*

Repeat this routine as often as you like. It is a good idea to take notes during or immediately after the procedure, before any details are forgotten.

You can also learn how a stone is affecting you by carrying or wearing it for a couple of days and then leaving it behind for another couple of days. Experimenting in this way, you will gather more useful knowledge about your stones than you could ever glean from reading about them. At the same time, you will be developing your sensitivity to crystals.

Where do Crystals Come from?

Crystals are all around us, from sand and pebbles on the beach to the finely polished slabs decorating the façades of government buildings. For centuries precious stones have been collected from riverbanks and dug out of the sides of hills and mountains wherever erosion has uncovered the sparkling caves and crevices. We see crystals at the end of a long process. It often takes millions of years before they emerge into the light of day.

(From top): *Rubellite in lepidolite forms in a pegmatite; citrine results from superheated solution; hematite is created when certain minerals are broken down by water.*

SLIDING LAYERS

The planet Earth appears firm, solid, and stable, but in reality, the solid rock continents upon which we live are only the thinnest of skins covering a turbulent, swirling, and dynamic interior. The planet's own rotation, its orbit around the sun, and the influence of the moon and other planets all create huge gravitational forces within the massive volumes of rock in the Earth's mantle. These layers slide over each other in a continuous movement.

CRYSTALLIZATION

Stresses can fracture the brittle layers of rock in the Earth's crust. This is where crystals can form, as heated gases and liquids under huge pressures force their way upward toward the surface, together with hot molten rock known as magma. These solutions are saturated with different elements and compounds—water, oxygen, sodium, gold, and iron, for example—that have dissolved from the deep layers within the mantle. As they pass through cooler, less active layers of rock, these elements fall out of solution and begin to crystallize in cavities and crevices. Depending on the mix of elements and environmental conditions, different minerals will form. The original amount of each raw material will determine the size of the crystals and the extent of each deposit.

Although not all crystals form in these volcanic, or igneous, conditions, many of the most precious gemstones do form in this way. These are usually the harder stones, such as garnet, ruby, and diamond. The borders of igneous activity around volcanoes are known as rich areas of mineralization.

ALTERED CONDITIONS

As the Earth's crust is in a state of continuous—albeit slow—change, conditions can alter, allowing successive waves of crystallization. Where rocks and minerals are changed into completely new structures and compositions by this successive crystallization, the conditions are called metamorphic. Metamorphic rocks and their attendant crystals occur in areas of great heat and pressure, often where rocks are buried, folded, and compressed by the Earth's movements.

As soon as they are exposed to water, wind, and ice, all rocks will begin to erode. Tons of rock particles are washed down rivers every day, settling in mud banks or being carried to the sea. Over millions of years, these deposits build up to an enormous thickness. Their weight, combined with that of the water above them, compresses the layers together to form another type of rock: sedimentary. Sedimentary rock tends to be more delicate than crystals that have formed under volcanic or metamorphic conditions.

CRYSTAL CHARACTERISTICS

No matter where they form, all crystals have the same basic characteristics. Furthermore, any mineral or chemical compound can form crystals, given the right conditions, and every mineral's crystals will have the same arrangement of constituent atoms throughout, which will be reflected in the geometric shapes visible in its faces, sides, and angles.

Crystal sizes range from extremely

small to several feet long. Rose quartz crystals, for example, are microscopically small (or microcrystalline); they take what is called massive form, where small crystals intergrow. With this type of crystal, no regular geometrical shapes can be seen. Many members of the quartz family are microcrystalline, usually because they form from solution in relatively low temperatures, and thus do not have the energy to form large crystals.

CRYSTAL FORMATION

Crystals will form wherever they have space to grow and, wherever possible, each will grow away from other crystals nearby. Seed crystals will begin to form on the surrounding bedrock or matrix. Very often, a microcrystalline layer appears first, before larger, separate crystals eventually emerge.

Where hot magma remains at a constant temperature for a long time, very large crystals can grow. This formation is known as a pegmatite. Many different sorts of minerals may crystallize along the length of a pegmatite, and some may even intergrow. Where there is a hollow space that is an enclosed bubble originally created by gas or liquid, mineral-rich solutions can seep in and crystallize. Depending on the conditions, either large crystals or layers of small microcrystalline crystals can grow here. These geodes, as they are called, are the main sources of amethyst, as well as other banded agates.

COLOR VARIATION

The variations in crystal color derive from minuscule amounts of different elements that create impurities within the crystal structure. In most instances, color is created when these small impurities alter the internal structure of the crystal so that light rays are bent toward one or the other end of the spectrum. In fact, to the confusion of the novice, most crystals can form in a wide range of different colors; this confusion is amplified when the same mineral is given a different name, depending on its color.

Learning to recognize the habit of a mineral—the common ways in which the crystals form together, their range of shapes and colors, and how they look both in a natural form and as a polished gemstone—is all part of familiarizing oneself with the energy of crystals.

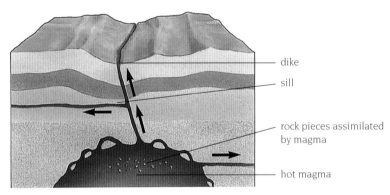

▲ **Rich mixtures** *Magma can give birth to many kinds of crystals as it cools and interacts with the native rock in many ways, each subtly changing the magma's chemical composition.*

▶ **Veins** *rich in minerals such as gold and iron are formed when hot magma packed with minerals seeps upward through cracks.*

▶▶ **Meteoric water** *Many crystals form when water is heated by magma underground and becomes enriched with minerals.*

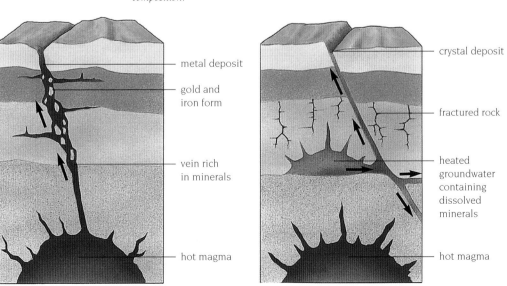

Crystal Energy

Humankind has been using crystals and minerals for millenia, and they continue to be integral to our lives today. Not only do we find them in complex machinery, engines, gauges, satellites, and space shuttles, but they are also used for making dyes, paints, and medicines. They even form part of our diets, as salt.

▲ Many everyday items, including watches and radios, depend upon quartz crystals to function efficiently.

STRUCTURE AND FORM

The special qualities of crystals—that which makes them visually fascinating and technologically useful—arise from the way in which they are formed, deep within the planet. When crystals begin to grow out of superheated solutions, their constituent atoms are free to combine, and do so in the most stable arrangements possible. Each crystal quickly builds up a characteristic three-dimensional pattern of atoms called a crystal lattice, which repeats itself throughout the entire crystal structure until there are no more free atoms available. As the availability of raw materials declines, the lattice begins to reduce in size. The regular prismatic sides form the points and terminations of the crystals.

Crystals are the most stable forms of matter in the universe. Having grown into their ideal solid forms, they possess energy that derives from their essential orderliness. Comfortable in their atomic arrangement, crystals are excellent at resisting external energies. For example, when their structure is compressed, many crystals will emit the resultant excess energy as light or an electric charge. Conversely, if an electric current is fed into a crystal, the crystal will respond by expanding slightly to accommodate the extra energy input.

An alternating current will create a regular pulsing in the structure of a quartz crystal. This energy has been used to replace the clockwork mechanism of watches, although today, the quartz used is usually artificial.

▲ Although the crystal lattice is invisible to the human eye, the arrangement of its atoms defines the visible shape of each crystal and affects its corresponding energies.

▲▶ Many of our most impressive technological developments are dependent upon crystal and mineral components in order to function properly.

RAYS OF LIGHT

A crystal's lattice structure determines how light will pass through, or between, its atoms. Some minerals—quartz, for example—allow rays of light to pass through almost unchanged, although the light does slow down fractionally. Other crystals split light into different beams, creating a polarizing effect. Tourmaline, for example, shows different colors, depending on the angle from which it is viewed. Calcite bounces light back off its surfaces to create a double image, called double refraction.

The behavior of light when it encounters a crystal lattice often produces the crystal colors we see. With transparent or translucent crystals, the resulting intense coloration introduces a very particular energy into the environment—whether into a room or into a person's energy field or aura. No other natural material can focus and concentrate the frequencies of light in such a consistent way.

NATURAL ENERGY RESONATORS

The behavior of crystals can be explained in terms of physics—particularly the area of solid-state physics that deals with energies at subatomic levels—but it is unwise to make direct comparisons to their uses in the contexts of healing and spiritual growth. Only some very tentative suggestions can be offered.

Crystals are the most orderly and also the simplest solid matter in the universe. Orderliness and simplicity in any form always brings chaotic energies into a greater state of order; this phenomenon is known as the principle of resonance. Crystals can be thought of as natural energy resonators. While there is no evidence that a crystal brought into the energy field of a human body changes the state of either the crystal or the body, some crystal healers believe that the dynamism of the body recognizes the crystal's orderly simplicity. According to this view, the crystal acts as a template against which the body's self-regulatory functions can perform more efficiently, encouraging a move toward health or clarity of perception.

The most changeable and volatile of human energy systems are the emotions and the thought processes. Sensitive people can perceive these energies as great swirls of colors which surround the body, like constantly changing patterns of weather. It is in the emotions that stress and imbalances build up and eventually upset the physical functions of the body. As coherent resonators, crystals can be very effective tools for releasing emotional stress and restoring calm to anxious individuals.

▶ *Whether a crystal is in its natural geometrical form, has been damaged by erosion, or has been shaped by humans, the internal structure of the crystal lattice ensures that the crystal will energize its surroundings.*

Healing Powers of Crystals

Today, crystal healing is looked upon by many as one of the more bizarre manifestations of the alternative scene. Its reputation has not been helped by the rather fabulous—and unsubstantiated—claims by some of its more outspoken promoters, such as the declaration that crystals were used in Atlantis. Indeed, many who claim to practice crystal therapy think that this is the only validation the therapy needs in order to be accepted! In reality, anthropological and historical evidence reveal that crystals have been valued as healing tools for thousands of years.

▲ *Setting gemstones in their appropriate metal enhances the power of both subjects. According to Ayurvedic tradition, a gold ring set with rubies will bring the energy of the sun to the wearer.*

AYURVEDIC TRADITIONS

Perhaps the oldest recorded, and most sophisticated, system using gemstones for healing is found in the Ayurvedic traditions of India. Many of the later ideas found in Europe during the Middle Ages derived from India by way of Arabic traders who, during the centuries of the Islamic expansion into southern Europe, reintroduced many of the classical texts on science and learning. Old Indian texts describe the origin of gemstones and define their beneficial powers. In one version, a demon sacrifices himself in order to prevent the destruction of the universe. From his remains all the precious gemstones were created. This correlation between body parts and crystals encourages the idea that ailments in certain organs can benefit from specific stones.

Other creation myths tell how the light from the creator focuses on each of the seven planets. The crystals in the Earth, in turn, gather and concentrate this energy to radiate planetary influences into their surroundings. Here we see the origin of the concept of crystals being linked to the stars and planets.

In ancient medicine, everything within the known universe had corresponding reflected energies within the human body. In this way, diagnoses of disease and healing was combined with knowledge of astronomy, astrology, the elements, herbs, and gemstones. In Ayurvedic gem therapy, difficulties arising from the position of the planets at the time of birth are assessed, thus showing where health problems may arise. Harmful influences can be reduced or even eliminated by wearing the gemstone that balances the negative trends.

In Ayurvedic tradition, the planets are ascribed specific gemstones of the finest quality and size. These are to be worn next to the skin, set in the appropriate metals. Not only should the gemstones be flawless and cut for brilliance, but they must also be prepared with the requisite number of mantras at the most auspicious times.

CLASSICAL INTERPRETATIONS

In Classical Greece and Rome, and later during the Middle Ages, gemstones were related to the virtues and vices of the planets. For example, red and orange stones such as carnelians and agates were associated with courage, honor, and success under the influence of the planet Mars. In magical and medical theory, stones would come under the influence of certain planetary spirits, and were best worked with during the appropriate day or hour. For example, magical works related to the moon (which rules the signs of Cancer and Pisces and the element of water) would best be performed on Mondays, or during the hour of day or night which came under the moon's influence. Silver, pearl, and moonstone would be used.

In many cultures, amulets and talismans have long been used to ward off harm, and to encourage success and virtue. Many types of materials are used, but gemstones are the most common. Even the regalia of emperors, kings, and priests are often studded with impressive jewels. Traditionally, this ornamentation not only displayed their wealth; it was also thought that by wearing the stones, their associated virtues and powers would influence the behavior of the wearer.

THE POWERS OF QUARTZ

Quartz, or rock crystal, has long played an important role in many cultures as a tool for healing and divination. Among the native tribes of North America, for example, quartz crystals were traditionally used to forecast the outcome of a hunt or battle. The stone would either be gazed into, like a crystal ball, in search of indications of success or failure; or it would be held in sunlight, and the reflected light was interpreted in accordance with where it fell.

In some traditions, healers would use quartz to examine a patient. The areas of disease, once located, were removed by rubbing the crystal over the body to draw out the imbalances. In such cases, it was the spirit of the stone that became the means of healing, and it was the spirit who was propitiated before, and thanked after, the healing session.

In Indonesia and Australasia, quartz is the primary stone used for divination and conversing with the spirits. The Aborigines of Australia use quartz as a symbolic means of initiation into healing and sorcery. Across the Pacific islands, quartz is regarded as belonging to the realm of the spirits, ancestors, and creator gods.

stones to place on and around the body to remove illness, but these are more often ordinary-looking rocks and pebbles than mineral crystals.

The placing of stones on and around the body for healing purposes seems to be an amalgamation of ideas from different traditions. Knowledge from India and Tibet on the subtle anatomy of the human body—particularly the seven main chakra centers—has been combined with color therapy theories that connect parts of the body with each of the colors of the rainbow spectrum. This interpretation seems to have occurred as a result of translations done in the early nineteenth and twentieth centuries of Indian texts by the Theosophical Society, who combined these texts with cross-cultural spiritualism. In another method of healing, crystals are used to direct or amplify healing energy that flows from or through the healer into the patient's auric field—a sort of supercharged spiritual healing.

All of these contemporary healing methods, along with the popular use of jewelry and birthstone amulets, continue our centuries-old relationship with the subtle energies of crystals and gemstones.

▲ *Encrusting symbolic religious items with gemstones adds to their magical power as well as their appearance.*

CEREMONIES AND RITUALS

In ancient times, certain stones clearly held important places in ceremony and everyday ritual. Coral, carnelian, turquoise, abalone shell, and obsidian were used throughout the Americas as protective amulets. In Central America, turquoise and jade were the favored materials to offer as ritual ornaments to the temple gods.

HEALING METHODS

There is little evidence that crystals are used as healing tools today in the same ways in which they were used in ancient times. Contemporary reports from Tibet and Peru suggest that some healers do use

▶ *Healers and shamans use a wide variety of tools to help them communicate with the spirits. In some traditions, stones or crystals are used.*

Divination

Divination is a way of clearing a straight, clear path to the future by paying attention to details and events so small as to escape ordinary notice, or to be thought irrelevant. In the world of divination, we learn that nothing is unimportant because all things are, at some level, interconnected. Like ripples on the surface of a pool that indicate activity out of sight, the diviner reads the world for signs of underlying energies that will shape future events or lives. Another method of obtaining information about the future is to ask those who know. The ancestors, gods, and spirits are thought to have a broad view of existence, and thus much traditional divination uses trance or similar altered-consciousness techniques to obtain advice from the spirit worlds. The two methods of foreseeing the future can sometimes be combined by asking the spirits to reveal their messages in the throw of dice or the fall of stones. Whatever the method used, success will come only when the mind enters the realm of timelessness.

Traditions and Techniques

Diviners are, by and large, practical people who, once their skills have been honed, are able to use whatever materials are at hand, whether it be bones, stones, dice, or a candle flame. Effective methods are passed down through tradition, but the most important tool of the trade is the mind of the diviner. All of the casting techniques, props, and prayers are useless unless they help the diviner achieve the state of awareness that is necessary in order to interpret the signs correctly.

▶ *The fall of objects such as nutshells or bones has long been used as a device to divine the will of the gods.*
▼ *The striking beauty of crystals suggests that they come from or can access the realm of the spirits.*

ANCIENT METHODS

Because historical and archaeological records regarding ancient crystal casting are incomplete, it can be difficult to correctly interpret the past uses to which various artifacts have been put. For example, a string of beads may have been worn as a decorative necklace, but the owner may also have used the beads to divine, as some cultures did. In the ancient Tibetan system of divination, called *Mo*, after the questioner asks the question and repeats the necessary mantras, beads are counted back in groups, leaving a maximum of six beads. Each number of remaining beads from one to six has a meaning ranging from "excellent" to "terrible," and thus the questioner is informed as to the likely outcome of the venture.

Crystals have long been used as a way of communicating with the spirit worlds and, through scrying (the act of gazing into a crystal ball), of looking into a window to the future. Natural crystals, polished spheres, and smooth mirrored surfaces have all been used in divination. Ordinary stones have likewise played a major role in divination techniques, especially the casting technique.

CASTING TECHNIQUES

Whereas scrying (meaning "seeing") opens the clairvoyant faculties of the diviner's mind, casting techniques follow predetermined rules of interpretation.

Casting divination techniques can take three main forms. In the simplest methods, the cast items have no significance or individual meaning. Very often there is a simple heads-or-tails approach, with shells or nuts landing on one side or the other. The various combinations provide the answer to the question at hand. The African system of *Ifa*, the Chinese *I Ching*, and some types of geomancy fall within this category.

In the second type of casting, each object has a specific and identifiable set of meanings. The way that each item falls in relation to the others creates a picture of which energies are involved with each other, suggesting the likely outcome. The Germanic runes, and possibly the Celtic systems of Coelbran, used this method.

Similarly, the bone oracles of South Africa employ a series of different items, the precise fall of which indicates a set outcome.

The third method of casting involves a set grid or map onto which the objects are cast. Each segment of the grid or map is ascribed a definite meaning. The cast object's fall can be interpreted either from where it lands or, in more complex systems, from the specific meaning given to each object, which is then modified by where it falls in the casting area. In the art of geomancy (literally "divination by earth"), for example, not only is the dispersion of the stones or the number of marks made important—the places where they fall or occur upon a set of predetermined grids is the key element. The use of a specially designed board for casting—the Astrological or Compass designs, for example (see pages 32-35 and 40-43)—allows for a precise interpretation for each placement.

PLAYING WITH TIME

Humanity's confusion— the very reason why there is a need for oracles at all—is caused by our experience of time as a linear flow, from past, to present, to future. We exist in the present and can remember the past, but the future can only be guessed at. We always seem to be heading into the unknown. And yet, in other states of awareness, time is more elastic and flexible. In dreams, for example, the past, present, and future interact within their own form of logic, echoing the essential secret of divination: it is possible to free the mind from the limits of the ordinary universe. In other words, the mind, not being a physical entity, is not constrained by the laws of time and space.

Our experience of time is very much tied to our metabolic rate—the speed of our lives. For a creature with a rapid metabolism, such as a rabbit, an hour might seem to stretch out forever, because so much activity is crowded into that time.

For a being with a slower metabolism—a tree, for example—a year might seem equivalent to our notion of a single day.

Crystals are the most stable matter in the universe. Once created, if left alone, they can remain in the same form for millenia. What experience of time do crystals have? Probably one of seeing the entire history of humankind flash by in a minute! In this way, crystals are quite removed from the flow of time. They are also free from the constraint of space: although each crystal is unique in form, its internal structure is constant in all samples of that mineral, wherever they are found across the universe.

◀ and ▼
For creatures of the animal kingdom, the flow of real time is experienced as body time. Small animals such as butterflies have rapid metabolic rates, and thus shorter life spans, whereas large animals such as elephants have slower metabolic rates, resulting in longer life spans.

The Principles of Crystal Reading

The principles of all oracles and divination are derived from the ancient world view of our tribal ancestors, who observed that all things and all events were inextricably tied together in a complex web of interaction. To most people at most times, this web is impossible to comprehend. But at certain special times—and for people with the ability to step between worlds and glimpse the web—it is possible to see how some strands interconnect.

▲ *In many cultures, the spider represents the creator goddess, weaving the world from her body.*
▶ *Carl Jung was an important influence on the development of contemporary interest in divination and the powers of the mind.*

SPIRITS AND THE UNCONSCIOUS

In the primeval world view, everything has a spirit, and everything is alive. What most of us perceive to be going on in the world is often only an outer, visible indication of a reality that exists within a greater spiritual world. Therefore, if one can learn to pose the right questions to the spirits in the correct manner, why should they not answer?

In his study of the unconscious, the psychologist Carl Jung explored the idea of a universal web, as well as the occurrence of simultaneous significant events with no apparent causal link. Modern research has also highlighted aspects of the universal web theory in the phenomenon known as the "hundredth monkey." This phenomenon occurs when a threshold number of individuals within a species—one in one hundred—has learned something new. Once this proportion of individuals has learned the new information, it appears that the information transfers to the entire population virtually instantly. Similarly, physics and mathematics have uncovered the chaos theory, which shows that seemingly random events reveal endless complexities of orderly patterning.

The inner mind, otherwise known as the unconscious—or that part of ourselves not usually noticed in the everyday rambling thought processes of conscious awareness—is able to access some of this underlying pattern-making at an intuitive level. However, linear thought cannot exist at this level of awareness, so messages must be sent in another form. Our unconscious mind speaks to our conscious mind by making us notice seemingly insignificant events, or by making connections, associations or symbolic links. These connections, associations, or links can reveal underlying patterns that may determine future events which will materialize into our conscious reality.

LEARNING TO DIVINE

Learning to divine is all about learning how to dip into nonverbal layers of awareness. A random casting of stones has no inherent meaning, so the conscious mind is left directionless. But the intuitive mind connects the question asked to the fall of stones, and can recognize significant patterns. It is then the job of the diviner to bring that information to the surface in a useful way.

In any reading, there will always be more than one possible interpretation. The beginner always frets about which one is right, but the answer to these worries is to let the meanings float up to your mind and go with whatever association comes up first. No one else can interpret your oracle for you because it is your mind that is the oracle—the stones, the board, and all other paraphernalia are simply tools that you can use to help you focus. The answers are within your mind, not in any divination object you are using. With practice, you will begin to recognize the feel of a correct interpretation.

◀ The human mind, in all its levels of perception, can comprehend much more than can the everyday conscious mind on its own. The diviner's brain is like a radio receiver that is able to tune into many of the different frequencies of the universe. The tools of divination simply help to focus his or her attention.

GIVING A SUCCESSFUL READING

The role of the diviner is to help clear up the confusion of the questioner—the person who has asked for the reading. If the questioner's confusion is lessened by the end of the session, then the session can be deemed a success, no matter how accurate the diviner feels the reading has been.

It is very important that in the reading process, both the diviner and the questioner are clear that this is not a test of clairvoyance, spiritual powers, or any other supernatural skill. Divining is not mind reading. The questioner should be open and willing to receive advice, and should be willing to provide whatever information the diviner needs to clarify the answer given by the cast.

The diviner also needs to take care how the interpretation is given. If you are the diviner, you must always remember that nothing is free from change. Even taking advice from a divination technique can significantly alter the likely outcome of any event. Avoid at all costs the curse of prophecy. Many mediocre and poor diviners insist that what they see will come to pass exactly as they see it. Where is free will in this interpretation? Where, indeed, are compassion and understanding? The diviner is there to advise, not to foretell. Foretelling is no different from cursing, because it sets up a strong tendency in the minds of both the diviner and questioner to work toward that outcome. Further, foretelling inextricably links the future actions of the questioner with the diviner, since the diviner has become a significant cause of those actions.

Divining should be a process of exploring possibilities. Clarity is the desired outcome, and both diviner and questioner should be working together toward this end. The web has infinite threads, along which anyone may travel. But a web is also full of holes that one can fall through. It is the job of the diviner to focus on the threads that may be of use in traversing the unknown voids of existence—not to distract the questioner with silly or trite observations.

Choosing Your Personal Stone

There are several guidelines that the questioner can follow when choosing a personal stone. The questioner can choose his or her own stone if doing the reading for him- or herself, or if the reading is done on his or her behalf by another. If the questioner will be absent during the reading, the diviner can choose a stone on his or her behalf.

The choice of a personal stone can be made in a number of ways. There are Eastern and Western systems in place that can be used as guidelines; or, one may choose not to follow any existing system, opting instead for an intuitive approach. All three methods are outlined in the next few pages.

◄▼ *Since ancient times, the zodiac signs have been associated with certain parts of the human body. In this way, each person becomes a tiny version of the universe.*

GEM	MAIN SIGNS	SECONDARY SIGNS	SIGNS THAT SHOULD AVOID THIS GEM
ruby	Leo	Aries	Libra, Aquarius
pearl	Cancer	Taurus	Scorpio, Capricorn
coral	Aries, Scorpio	Capricorn	Cancer, Libra, Taurus
emerald	Gemini, Virgo	Virgo	Pisces, Sagittarius
topaz	Sagittarius, Pisces	Cancer	Capricorn, Gemini, Virgo
diamond	Libra, Taurus	Pisces	Virgo, Aries, Scorpio
blue sapphire	Aquarius, Capricorn	Libra	Aries, Leo, Cancer
amethyst	Taurus		Scorpio
cat's-eye	Scorpio		Taurus

PLANET	BODY PART	ORIGINAL CRYSTALS	ACCEPTABLE SUBSTITUTES
Sun	blood	ruby	rose quartz, garnet, spinel, zircon
Moon	teeth	pearl	moonstone, quartz
Mercury	bile	emerald	aquamarine, peridot, jade, green tourmaline
Venus	bones	diamond	white stones
Mars	intestines	coral	carnelian, red jasper
Jupiter	skin	yellow sapphire	topaz, citrine
Saturn	eyes	blue sapphire	amethyst, lapis lazuli
Rahu (north node)	semen/ovum	hessonite garnet	
Ketu (south node)	sound	cat's-eye (chrysoberyl)	
	nails	tourmaline	
	sight/liver	lapis lazuli	
	whole body	agate	
	spleen	quartz	

EASTERN SYSTEMS

In the early Ayurvedic and Tantric texts, certain gems were related to specific parts of the human body. Wearing these gems was believed to help heal the relevant body parts, and to support an individual's progress in life. There were nine stones related to the planets and the nodes of the moon (points in space related to the movement of the moon and the apparent movement of the sun), with four extra stones related solely to the body.

The chart on the lower half of the facing page shows the planets and their corresponding body parts and crystals, plus acceptable substitutes. You can use it as a guideline when choosing your own personal stone, or if choosing a stone for a questioner for whom you will be divining. This system of choosing a stone is particularly useful if the questioner is having problems with any of the body parts named. The choice of the relevant crystal will help alleviate the illness.

Further Ayurvedic correspondences were linked to the signs of the zodiac. Certain gemstones are strongly connected to certain signs, with other secondary signs connected—albeit less strongly—to the gemstones as well. In this system, there are specific gems that should be avoided for each sign. The chart on the upper half of the facing page shows how to choose a stone using this system.

▲ *The present-day zodiac wheel, with its animals and figures, derives from the ancient Greeks.*
▼ *Birthstones are one of the ways in which we link the energies of the planet with the universe as a whole, and align ourselves with the cosmos.*

WESTERN SYSTEMS

In the West, as early as the fifth century AD, writers have linked the twelve stones that adorned the breastplate of the biblical Hebrew high priest to the twelve signs of the zodiac, and later to the twelve months of the year. But it was not until 1912, at a meeting of the U.S. National Association of Jewelers, in Kansas, that a general consensus was reached as to an agreed pairing of birthstones and crystals with months of the year and signs of the zodiac. The lists below are widely held to be the definitive guides.

MONTH	BIRTHSTONE	STAR SIGN	DATES	CRYSTALS
January	garnet	Aries	March 20–April 21	diamond, bloodstone, aquamarine, emerald
February	amethyst	Taurus	April 21–May 22	emerald, diamond
March	bloodstone, aquamarine, jasper	Gemini	May 22–June 22	pearl, moonstone, agate, emerald
April	diamond, sapphire	Cancer	June 22–July 23	ruby, emerald
May	emerald, agate	Leo	July 23–August 24	ruby, peridot, turquoise
June	pearl, moonstone, emerald	Virgo	August 24–September 23	opal, tourmaline, peridot
July	ruby, onyx	Libra	September 23–October 23	opal, tourmaline, sapphire, topaz
August	peridot, carnelian	Scorpio	October 23–November 23	topaz, opal, aquamarine
September	sapphire	Sagittarius	November 23–December 22	turquoise, garnet, topaz
October	opal, tourmaline, aquamarine	Capricorn	December 22–January 21	garnet, turquoise
November	topaz	Aquarius	January 21–February 19	amethyst, garnet, ruby, diamond, jade
December	turquoise, lapis lazuli, ruby	Pisces	February 19–March 20	aquamarine, bloodstone, amethyst, jasper

OTHER WAYS TO CHOOSE YOUR PERSONAL STONE

Following Eastern or Western guidelines is just one way of choosing your personal stone. There are currently a great many crystals that are easily available and, year by year, even more are finding their ways into our lives. You may thus wish to choose your personal stone by sight, instinct, after having undertaken research, or even randomly.

▼ *Choosing a personal stone by sight is both the easiest and most intuitive method, as we typically feel drawn to that stone which immediately attracts our attention.*

PREFERENCE

Arguably, the best reason for choosing a particular personal stone is because you like it. When we desire something, it is because seeing it creates changes in our internal chemistry, helping us to feel good. Having a particular preference gives each of us a means of showing our individuality. It is true that preferences change, and this could be an argument against choice as a way of determining a personal stone. However, since we are constantly changing and growing, it also makes sense that our personal stone should change along with us. Some people find their instinctive choice does in fact stay with them for the whole of their lives. Often such a stone reflects key factors of the individual's personality and behavioral patterns.

COLOR

Color is one of the greatest attractions of crystals. Our instinctive reaction to color is so automatic that it takes vigilance to detect the subtle changes when we encounter different colors. Some reactions tend to be emotional, ranging from "Delicious! I could eat it!" to "Get that out of my sight!"—and all points in between. The following method can help you instinctively choose a personal stone.

1. *Have before you a selection of stones.*
2. *Close your eyes and allow your breathing to settle.*
3. *Have the intention that, when you open your eyes, you will be drawn to a crystal that is appropriate for your personal stone.*
4. *Open your eyes and pay attention to where they come to rest.*
5. *The crystal upon which your gaze has fallen can become your personal stone.*

This method can be used to select personal stones for each reading. It can also be used to find stones that will help you over longer periods of time, or for particular purposes. Just make sure that you have a clear intention in your mind before you select your stone.

READING ABOUT THE QUALITIES OF STONES

Some people may prefer a more logical approach when choosing a personal stone. Over the last thirty or forty years, many books have been written detailing the qualities and possible uses of crystals. Reading about crystals in these sources is a good way to get an overall assessment of how they are commonly perceived by those who have studied their powers and properties.

If this method is chosen, it is a good idea to look at as many sources as possible. Some crystals will seem to match your personality characteristics quite closely; these would make useful personal stones. Another approach is to select your stone according to the qualities that you wish to develop within yourself. If you wish to improve your patience, for example, a dark blue stone would be your best choice, and you would be well advised to steer clear of red, orange, and yellow stones. See pages 44-135 to find out the characteristics associated with each of the stones featured in this book.

RANDOM SELECTION

A random choice of a personal stone can be ideal for doing readings, or even just for choosing a stone for the day. The following two methods work particularly well.

METHOD ONE

1. Place all your stones inside a cloth bag.
2. Relax and slow your breathing down.
3. Have in your mind a clear intention to find a personal stone for the reading or for that day.
4. Dip your hand into the bag and pull out one stone.
5. If you like, you can look up the stone you have chosen in a book on crystals; it may provide you with relevant advice or guidance.

METHOD TWO

1. Cut or tear as many small pieces of paper as you have stones.
2. Write your name on one piece of paper, shuffle all the papers and then lay them face down.
3. Place a stone on top of each of the pieces of paper.
4. When every piece of paper has a stone on it, turn each paper over until you find the one with your name under it. This can be your personal crystal, or your crystal for the day. Look up the meaning associated with your chosen crystal in a book on crystals for additional insight.

▲ *There is no such thing as chance in a divinatory reading. Where a random process links a person's name with a stone, there is significance in that combination.*

Preparing for Divination: Setting the Scene

CLEANSING YOUR CRYSTALS

Before you do any work with your crystals, they need to be cleansed to ensure that they are free of all outside influences and energies. Most hard crystals (from 3 or above on the Mohs scale, which indicates the relative hardness of minerals) can be safely washed in slightly soapy water to remove grime, dust, and fingerprints. After washing a stone, rinse it well with clean water and allow it to dry naturally in the open air. It is best to keep it out of strong sunlight.

Softer crystals may dissolve or become damaged by washing, and so other methods of cleansing will be necessary. Below are a variety of alternatives to cleansing using soap and water.

SOUND

Another easy cleansing method involves the use of bells, hand cymbals, or singing bowls. Sound of a fine quality and piercing resonance will help the crystals release any negative energy. If placing crystals in a singing bowl, put a small piece of fabric in the bottom to help stop them from rattling together when the bowl sings.

WATER

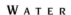

Crystals that are not water-soluble can be held under running water. The intention is to release any negative energies, and to return them to a place where they can be used constructively.

INCENSE

Incense is an easy and effective cleansing method. Each stone can be passed through the smoke several times. Traditional purifying incenses, such as sandalwood, frankincense, and pine, are popular, as are the white sage and cedars traditionally used by Native Americans to cleanse their ritual spaces. Another option is to tie dried lavender stalks together and burn them, as they give off a pleasing aromatic smoke. The burning of bay leaves makes a pungent cleansing smoke.

SALT

It is inadvisable to use salted water for cleansing, as the salt crystals lodge in the crevices of the crystals being cleansed and can dull some surfaces. Dry sea salt can, however, be used; simply pile it onto the crystals to be cleansed and leave for 24 hours. (Don't use the salt for cooking afterwards!)

PREPARING THE PHYSICAL SPACE

The space in which the reading will take place can be as simple or as ornate as you wish. Following a specific routine can be very useful in setting the scene. Here are some suggestions for you to consider:

1. Whether you do your readings in bright or dim surroundings is really a personal decision. When we are relaxed and secure, the intuitive faculties work best, so decide what you feel most comfortable with.

2. You may want to have a small lamp or lighted candle nearby.

3. Choose a cloth to go under the board. The color of the cloth is up to you. Black is the color most often connected with any sort of reading, although deep reds and golds can be more welcoming.

4. Small objects such as flowers, talismans, or spiritual images may also feel appropriate in the space.

5. If you will be divining using a divinatory board, you may want to make a decision about which direction the board will face when you read. This consideration is particularly apt for the Compass board (see page 32). For example, you may prefer to align the North position on the board to the north of the room. You may also have a preference as to where you will sit.

6. Think about how your crystals are going to be presented— in an open display, or in a closed bag or box.

FINAL CONSIDERATIONS

When the scene is set, light some incense and leave the room to prepare yourself. Make sure that you will not be disturbed by the telephone or doorbell, or by any children or pets. Light the candle or switch on the lamp as you sit down to do the reading.

When the reading is finished, snuff out the candle or switch off the lamp. Clear away all your tools, then cleanse your crystals. Light some more incense if you wish, then leave the room empty for a while.

▼ *Choose items that will help you relax your mind and create a sacred space for your reading. As sacred space is naturally removed from our normal experience of time and space, it helps to facilitate the divination process.*

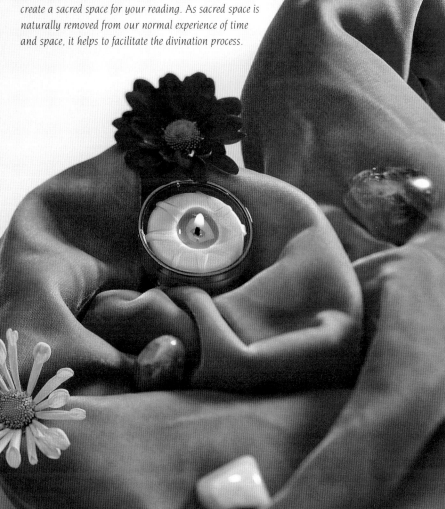

Preparing for Divination: Balancing Your Mental State

Preparation by the diviner, whatever the divination method, is the single most important factor that will influence the clarity and accuracy of a reading. Along with the preparation of the physical space, mental preparation is essential.

CENTERING AND GROUNDING

In the realm of divination, centering and grounding are essential for protecting and supporting the diviner. It is advisable to do these exercises both before and after a reading. Done before the reading, they help to set the scene, taking the diviner into a secure personal space; done after a reading, they help to anchor the diviner safely back into normal awareness. If a series of readings is being done, particularly for different people, these techniques can be used in between readings to clear any residual energies, enabling you to start afresh.

CENTERING

All centering techniques bring personal energies to a point of balance and rest. This helps to create enough detachment from the surroundings to create clarity of the mind, and to balance the energies of the body to encourage the easy flow of information and intuition. Here is one particularly effective centering technique.

1. *Sit still for a few moments, allowing your body and breathing to settle.*
2. *Take your attention to your breath, and then to your spine.*
3. *Imagine your breath traveling up and down your spine about five to ten times.*
4. *Leaving the breath, direct your attention to your spine, as if it were the only part of your body.*
5. *After a few minutes, bring your awareness back to the present.*

You can use also the "tapping-in" procedure, as described in the section on pendulum dowsing (see step 2, page 37), to center yourself.

◀ *Taking a few moments to become calm and relaxed allows intuitive skills to come to the fore. Mental neutrality and a calm emotional state are both essential for a successful reading.*

GROUNDING

Grounding links the diviner into the vast resources of the planet. This connection ensures ample provision of the raw, manifesting energy necessary for a good reading. It also protects the integrity of the reader's personal energy, removing the possibility of absorbing negativity, especially when reading for someone else. Below is a time-tested technique for grounding called "growing roots."

1. *Sit still for a moment or two, allowing your body and breathing to settle.*
2. *Direct your attention to your feet.*
3. *Imagine roots growing out of your feet and spreading into the earth.*
4. *On each out-breath, allow the roots to extend outward.*
5. *On each in-breath, feel the energy and stability from the earth filling the whole of your body.*
6. *After a minute or two, bring your awareness back to the present.*

Grounding can be done immediately after you have centered your energy. It can also be done at any time during a reading if either party is tired or their concentration has wandered or weakened.

DEDICATION

Most diviners like to dedicate their work before they begin, although this is largely a matter of personal taste and conscience. In its simplest form, a dedication can be a simple request for guidance to the universe as a whole. Or, it can become as elaborate as needed. Above all, any dedication must make sense and be relevant to the diviner. For example, if you are familiar with Native American traditions, it may be appropriate to dedicate your work to one of the Native American spirits. If you don't adhere to any specific set of beliefs, however, then a dedication to the highest and finest energies of light may meet your needs. Whatever dedication is chosen, it must be done with awareness and faith. Paying lip service to the subject of the dedication will only distort the flow of energy through the body.

APPEARANCE

Over the years, the media have created stereotypes of clairvoyants and mediums with great panache, to the extent that the public often expects to see these people dressed in a specific costume. That said, it may well be that dressing in certain colors or styles helps create a persona that is easy to work behind. It certainly provides an excellent excuse to be dramatic!

You may want to consider your dress and overall appearance when doing a reading. Wearing a certain ring or shirt can become part of the ritual preparation, and a talisman for skilled work. However, it is also worth considering the impact of certain styles of dress and appearance on the questioner (if you are doing a reading for another person). Whereas some people might be impressed by a black cloak and rich embroidery, others may feel very uncomfortable in your presence.

COMPLETION

When you have finished doing the reading, it is a good idea to have a routine that draws a clear line between reading time and everyday life. Below are some suggested techniques to signal the completion of the reading.

- Centering and grounding are both essential after a reading.
- If you have had a light on or a candle lit, then switch it off or snuff it out.
- Fold up the board and cloth.
- Cleanse the crystals.
- Many people find it helpful to wash their hands as both a literal and symbolic gesture of separation.
- If you have on "work clothes," remember to change out of them.

▲ *Adopting a dramatic appearance can set the divination session apart from everyday life, making it easier for you to work and focusing the attention of the questioner on what you are saying.*

Methods of Crystal Reading

There are many ways of divining using crystals. In this section
we look at some of the most popular methods: casting crystals on
a divinatory board, scrying, and pendulum dowsing.

THE COMPASS BOARD

The Compass board is a divinatory tool
that, when crystals are cast upon it, can
help clarify the questioner's present and
future. When cast upon the board, the
position of the fallen crystals—combined
with each crystal's unique divinatory
properties—are read by the diviner, who
interprets them for the questioner. With
this divinatory board, the directions of the
compass provide the guidelines for the
interpretations (see pages 38-39 for how
crystals are cast, and pages 40-41 for
a description of how the Compass board
is used).

Evidence shows that ancient cultures
found magical and ritualistic significance
in the four directions of the compass. The
passage of the sun through the sky was a
measure of time, and the directions in
which the sun and stars rose and set
became an integral part of ritual and
religious life. Each culture had its own
descriptions of the directions, which were
linked with gods and goddesses, animals,
and the elements. The following descriptions are an amalgamation of Chinese,
Native American, and Celtic traditions.

NORTHWEST

This direction primarily covers social interactions and situations in which we want to help others. People who are
helpful to us are shown here as well, such as those we
regard as teachers or advisers—as are those who
share our ideals. Social interactions may result in
friction, however, so this direction can imply
caution. Travel is also dealt with here.

WEST

Considerations of the west begin with looking after ourselves physically—taking care of
our bodies. Talents that need nurturing can
also make an appearance. Anything that can
be considered valuable to us and which might
benefit from extra care, such as children or
our planet, are also placed here in the west.
However, the drive to care for something can
become overpowering—even destructive—if
there are too many demands placed on the
nurturing that we can provide. Choices can
thus also be part of the west, with the added
difficulty of having to choose between things
we care about. The joy of living and the happiness that comes from watching those in our
care flourish also belongs here.

SOUTHWEST

The southwest covers all aspects of relationships, emphasizing those with emotional
ties. This is a very receptive direction, showing that we absorb emotions from others. The
southwest is particularly about love—both for
ourselves and for others. Love is an emotion
that ebbs and flows, and requires flexibility.
Even in very secure relationships, partners
tend to fall in and out of love with one another continuously. The greatest challenge in a
relationship is to allow the other person to be
themselves. This direction is all about bringing security and trust to our relationships.

NORTH

Talents come together in the north, creating the flowering of personal potential. Time and patience are needed, however, for a full realization of this potential, and we must be able to accept and work with our own vulnerabilities and weaknesses. Without this acceptance, we have no firm ground upon which to stand.

NORTHEAST

The northeast is concerned with expanding the boundaries of knowledge. For those driven by the need to improve themselves or their situations, this direction covers education in all its forms, from day-to-day discoveries to philosophical concepts. One facet of self-improvement is taking time out to be with your own thoughts. Times of stillness and self-reflection also belong to this direction.

EAST

The east deals with issues surrounding the family, as well as with relationships between groups of individuals who function like a family. Questions of responsibility arise, along with the fine boundary that separates nurturing from smothering and freedom from restriction. On the negative side of the boundary, the emotional stress produced by large amounts of responsibility can cause a myriad of health problems. Changes in mental approaches to these issues can help a great deal, as can increased and more effective communication—a vital factor in healthy families.

SOUTHEAST

The southeast is associated with all aspects of wealth. Most people associate the term wealth with money, (and this direction certainly covers this form of wealth), but here we refer as well to other things that create a feeling of prosperity. For some people, this will be health, children, happiness, or friends; for others, the accumulation of possessions will suffice. This direction also relates to natural beauty, and to harmony. It can show an instinctive grasp of how life in general works, and of being in tune with the world.

◀◀ On the Atlantic shores of Europe, stone circles were set up so that ancient inhabitants could accurately predict the passage of ritual time.

SOUTH

The south is associated with recognition for the effort which we have put into our work. To achieve any level of success usually requires persistence, stubbornness, and a fair helping of luck. Faith in the workings of the world is needed to make new starts, with no certainty of the outcome. Speaking the truth is an important facet of the energies in the south. This suggestion is primarily directed toward oneself, for if a person deceives him- or herself, a price must be paid.

THE ASTROLOGICAL BOARD

Based on the astrological houses, the Astrological board is another popular divinatory tool upon which crystals can be cast (see pages 38-39 for how crystals are cast, and pages 42-43 for a description of how the Astrological board is used). The astrological houses are numbered subdivisions of the astrology circle, and indicate where in an individual's life certain energies are evident. As with the Compass board, the position of the fallen crystals—combined with each crystal's divinatory properties—are read by the diviner.

1ST HOUSE

This house shows how the questioner appears to others. It can indicate as well which needs are paramount for the questioner's survival. It also shows the qualities that the questioner must learn to accept in him- or herself.

2ND HOUSE

Our values and the ways in which they shape our world are paramount in this house. These values fall into two main categories. The first category deals with the value we place on integrity, whereas the second category relates to the way we attract money and our attitude toward it.

3RD HOUSE

This house encompasses short journeys. It also covers the way we communicate in everyday situations. It deals as well with relationships with siblings, and also with gossip and lack of secrecy. This house also suggests adopting a more easygoing approach to life.

◀ *In this fifteenth-century calendar taken from a French medieval Book of Hours, the month of August is depicted with the sun in between the first house (Aries) and the sixth house (Virgo).*

4TH HOUSE

The roots of a problem or situation are shown here, and any hidden underlying concerns are hinted at. This house can give an indication of the emotional context of an issue, and insecurity here can lead to a great deal of fear. The home is another facet of the fourth house, so here we find residential moves and family changes. We also learn what someone expects of their home.

6TH HOUSE

Everyday work situations and health are both covered by this house. The skills someone brings to their work and the type of work they enjoy are defined here. Health indications here show where the body is accumulating stress.

7TH HOUSE

This house covers relationships—personal, professional, and public, and highlights relationship issues. It can also indicate the type of role someone typically plays in a public or professional context. Reactions to legal issues in a person's life are also shown here.

8TH HOUSE

Situations in which deep emotions are brought to the surface are evident in this house—death, birth, or a major life change, for example. Psychic skills enabling the transference of information can also surface here. Money queries also fall within the parameters of this house.

9TH HOUSE

The acquisition of knowledge is dealt with in this house. Broadcasting information through the media and learning through study or travel are all included here. Anything that extends the horizons of experience, including philosophical debate, is also present.

10TH HOUSE

This house indicates the status of a person in the eyes of the public. It also represents the way a person wants to be seen, and thus it can actually show a self-created image. It is a vehicle for ambitions and goals, and may also show what type of long-term planning needs to be done.

11TH HOUSE

Our friends and acquaintances and the activities that we enjoy in their company can be shown here. Our overall attitudes about our community are also aspects of this house, as is the willingness to serve without receiving any recognition for our efforts.

12TH HOUSE

The inner realms of the individual are often evident here. This is where hidden parts of our personality can sabotage our plans. To stop this self-undoing, we need to examine our unconscious through meditation and dreams and discover what is hidden there.

5TH HOUSE

At first glance, this house appears to be diverse, dealing with hobbies, children, pets, creativity, romance, and gambling. However, upon closer examination, there is a uniform thread that links all of these elements: enjoyment. Here we need to lighten up, enjoy life, and take a few risks. Romantic encounters, flirting, and unconditional relationships are also included here. This house also deals with our ability to express ourselves creatively.

SCRYING

The crystal ball is the archetypal trademark of the fortune-teller. Scrying—the art of gazing into a crystal ball and foretelling the future—is truly a way of seeing into other worlds. The skill involves the correct interpretation of the images that appear. A ball of rock crystal or glass has typically been the favored scrying tool, but many other items have been used as well: concave mirrors, shaped discs of black obsidian, bowls of water or ink, still pools—even thumbnails! Whatever object is used acts like a window through which the seer gazes. Scrying requires patience and persistence, but it is a useful mental exercise, even if full success is not realized.

A crystal sphere can be expensive, particularly if flawless, but it has the advantage over glass of being more conducive to stillness and a calm mind. A natural, unshaped crystal can also be used if it has a large facet that can be looked through. Obsidian spheres or large discs can also be good scrying tools. Below are some rules to follow to maximize your chances of scrying successfully.

- The scrying tool is a window upon which to rest the eyes and the mind. Set it up so that you can comfortably gaze into it without straining your body. Surrounding it with dark fabric is helpful, as this reduces the chance of distraction.
- Use subdued lighting, perhaps a candle, or even darkness. Position the scrying tool so that there are no reflections visible from where you sit.
- Close your eyes and focus on the purpose of your divination. Whatever you see or sense will in some way relate to your question, so the clearer your intention, the clearer your answer will be.
- Open your eyes and steadily gaze into the object. Do not focus on the surface, or even the interior; rather, use it as a window and look beyond it. Keep your gaze relaxed but fixed.
- With practice, a change will seem to occur after awhile. This is often described as a white mist or a swirling within the field of vision. At this point, it is important to remain focused on your intention, but stay relaxed and pay close attention to everything that occurs without focusing too much on anything—like looking at the stars with your peripheral vision, or at three-dimensional computer art.
- All that is perceived is within the mind's eye rather than in the mirror or ball, and so any mental disturbance will interrupt the vision.
- When you have practiced a number of times, bring your mind back to its normal focus by covering your scrying surface with a cloth, increasing the light, and grounding yourself (see pages 30-31). Scrying creates a trance-like state, so it is important to make sure that your sense of awareness returns to its normal functioning. Make notes of your experiences.

▼ *Whichever tool is chosen for scrying, it should help the diviner achieve an unfocused and receptive state of mind.*

PENDULUM DOWSING

Crystals make very useful pendulums. They can be mounted and suspended on a cord or chain, or placed inside a metal spiral. A pendulum works by amplifying the minuscule movements within the user to create a swing in the pendulum. These muscular movements are a physical response to the subtle energy changes in the body. The types of movement the pendulum displays, particularly for yes/no responses, are individual. It can take some time to become confident in deciphering pendulum responses.

PENDULUM PRACTICE

The practice exercise below is to show you that the pendulum will follow your eyes and your thoughts—if you let it. When using a pendulum to determine a yes/no response, your thoughts must be in neutral mode, and your eyes should not be focused on the pendulum; rather, they should be looking past it. If you focus your eyes directly on the pendulum and watch it closely, it will simply swing whichever way you will it to, and the divination will not be accurate.

- Find a crystal pendulum which suits you, both in terms of crystal type and weight. To find a weight of crystal with which you are comfortable, sample a selection of crystal sizes, swinging the pendulum to test how each weight feels.
- Using the arrows to the left as a guide, set the pendulum swinging over each arrow in turn, focusing on each arrow as you do so. You'll find that by watching the pendulum closely, you can will it to move in the directions of the arrows—a power you should not use when dowsing!

► *A pendulum can swing in many different ways. Once you have established a clear yes/no response, you can begin to identify more subtle response movements, such as "yes, but..." or "no, but perhaps later."*

FINDING YOUR PERSONAL YES/NO RESPONSE

Having chosen a pendulum with which you would like to work, follow the steps below to determine which way your pendulum will move to indicate "yes," and which way it will move to indicate "no."

1. Find a place where you will have no distractions, and settle yourself into a comfortable position.
2. With either hand, tap the top of your breastbone (thymus gland) lightly with your fingertips ten to fifteen times. This action temporarily balances the energies of the body, which helps to increase the accuracy of dowsing. (This procedure is known as "tapping in.")
3. With the pendulum in one hand, set it swinging in a forward–backward movement.
4. Cover your navel with your other hand (this links you directly into the center of the subtle energy system of the body).
5. Close your eyes.
6. Focus on the statement "Show me my 'yes' response."
7. After a short while, open your eyes and note how the pendulum is moving.
8. Repeat steps 2 through 5.
9. Focus again, this time on the statement "Show me my 'no' response."
10. After a short while, open your eyes and note the movement of the pendulum.

YOUR YES/NO RESPONSES

Make a note of how the pendulum swings to indicate "yes," and how it swings to indicate "no." If both response movements look the same, don't worry. Take a break for a few hours and then try again, allowing extra time for tapping in (see step 2, above right).

You are now ready to use your pendulum as a yes/no indicator. Before you get started, however, here are a few general points to keep in mind.

- If you have too much of an emotional investment in a specific possible outcome, accurate answers are unlikely.
- The questions posed need to have "yes" or "no" as a possible answer. For example, there is no point asking "Which day next week will the letter from Uncle Fred arrive?" It is necessary to break that question into a series of questions along the lines of "Is Uncle Fred's letter going to come on Monday?" If the answer is no, you would then repeat the question for each day of the week, until the answer is yes.
- If you ask a series of questions but seem to be getting nowhere, try re-examining your questions. Precise questions work best, while vague questions produce vague responses.

Casting and Interpreting Crystals

To make a full casting or reading, you will need at least thirteen different crystals. The stones should be no more than an inch (25mm) in length. Once you choose your crystals, it is best if you use them for divination only; this way, you will ensure that your readings maintain their sacredness and purity. Each time the stones are used, it is important to cleanse them before putting them away, and they should always be cleansed between readings. This will help to maintain the integrity and accuracy of your work. When not in use, the stones should be covered, to keep the dust away.

CASTING THE CRYSTALS

Casting can involve letting the crystals fall at random over the board, or it can mean placing them specifically and deliberately onto areas of the board. If the stones are thrown and some fall off of the board, this has implications for the interpretation. Here are some commonly used methods of casting crystals on a board.

▼ *Make sure your board is placed upon a surface that is large enough to catch any stones that may fall off the board when cast randomly.*

SHAKE AND THROW

Select a total of thirteen crystals from the stones that are available to you. You can include your personal stone in this number (see pages 24-27), or select thirteen stones in addition to your personal stone. If the crystals are small enough, collect them in your hands and gently shake them. While you are doing this, focus your thoughts on the question at hand. When the time feels right, release the crystals onto the board. Leave all of the stones where they land.

CASTING ONE BY ONE

Have your crystals close at hand, but keep them out of your direct sight, in a bag or box. Focus on the question at hand. Pick one crystal and cast it onto the board. Repeat this process until you have a total of twelve or thirteen crystals on the board. Cast your personal stone last. With this method, the subconscious mind adjusts slightly as each selection is made. This adjustment lends the reading a greater depth and accuracy, particularly if the issue is complex.

INDIVIDUAL PLACEMENT

Take a moment to focus on the empty board with your question in mind. Taking your focus to the first area where you want to place a stone—perhaps the area most relevant to the issue—pick a stone at random and place it within that area. Continue using the same procedure until every desired area has had a stone placed upon it. If your personal crystal is among your selections, place it in the center to complete the spread, or place it intuitively in one of the sections, for extra focus.

TARGETED READING

Referring to the crystal information pages contained herein (see pages 44–135), choose the thirteen stones that seem to best reflect the subject matter that is relevant to your question. These stones can be cast randomly onto the board, or you can use the individual placement method.

INTERPRETING THE CRYSTALS

Interpretation in any type of reading will make sense only if the question posed is kept in mind during the entire process, so that the information given relates to the relevant issue. For example, if the reading is about work, but it is interpreted in terms of romance, it will not be helpful, and will likely be misleading. The person doing the reading must sift through several possible interpretations of the reading, and then ascertain which interpretation is the relevant (i.e. correct) one for the questioner. The decision as to which interpretation is relevant is an intuitive one, and may be made by the diviner alone or in conjunction with the questioner. It is important to recognize that there is seldom a right or wrong interpretation, just different degrees of possibility.

Both the Compass and Astrological boards have their own key words, as do each of the crystals. When you begin to interpret a reading, start by putting the relevant sets of key words together. Both boards will tell you where in the life of the questioner the relevant energy or issue is likely to appear, while each of the crystals will explain which energy or issue is being highlighted.

Don't be disheartened if at first you find it hard to blend the key words together. The more readings you do, the easier reading becomes, and the more meanings you will be able to incorporate.

When using either board, it is a good idea to keep a written record of the question posed. This will help keep you focused, and will insure that your questions are concise.

CRYSTAL GROUPINGS

To refine your reading of the crystals, you should bear in mind certain supplementary insights offered by the positions of the crystals that have been randomly cast on the board. The following rules apply to crystals cast on both the Compass and Astrological boards.

Crystals falling some distance off the board: The energies suggested by these crystals are not at issue at this particular time, but may be more appropriate in about three months' time.

Crystals falling just off the board: The energies of these crystals are on the periphery of the question, and are likely to be part of the picture in two weeks' time.

Crystals over the edge of the board circle, partly in: These are influences incoming or outgoing during the next week; intuition may indicate which.

Crystals touching lines between directions or houses: These crystals will have influence in both areas they touch, so both will need to be considered.

Crystals touching each other in the same section: These crystals are inextricably linked together, and need to be interpreted as such.

Crystals touching each other in different sections: Both sections are seen as linked together through each of the crystal energies.

Crystals that are long and thin: These suggest linkage between the sections of the board they point toward.

Crystals falling at the center and/or touching the personal stone, if used: These crystals are tied in very closely with the questioner, and will represent very personal characteristics.

Groups of crystals: Where a bunch of crystals land in a group, the area that they occupy is emphasized.

INTERPRETING THE COMPASS BOARD

For those who are beginners at casting, the crystals on the board, once cast, can seem confusing, and their interpretation may seem like an overwhelming task. It is thus advisable to read the crystals in the sequence that appears below, starting from the south and ending with southeast. As you become more familiar with the board, and with the various ways in which the directions interact with the crystals, you will probably develop your own reading sequence.

See page 39 for the meaning of crystals that fall in the following ways:
● outside the boundaries of the board or partly in
● on lines between directions or houses
● touching each other in the same or different sections
● at the center of the board
● touching your personal stone
● pointing in a certain direction
● in groups

See also pages 44-135 for interpretations of specific crystals cast upon the board.

SOUTH
Crystals that land here show how to gain recognition. In questions concerning romance, look for crystals indicating persistence: these can help to get a relationship moving. Blue crystals here show a need to let things flow. Red crystals suggest the need to begin again.
Key words: Recognition, luck, beginnings, honesty

SOUTHWEST
Crystals that land here describe facets of any sort of relationship. Pink crystals address the questioner's input into the situation, whereas green crystals hint at the quality of the relationship.
Key words: Relationships, receptivity, flexibility, compassion, possessiveness

WEST
Crystals landing here highlight our capacity to fulfill our daily needs. This can extend to people or relationships that are in need of nurturing. Black, red, or clear crystals here may suggest that priorities need to be re-examined. Yellow or gold crystals hint at the need to develop personal skills.
Key words: Caring, physical needs, children, talents, pleasure

NORTHWEST

The northwest covers friends and community. Violet and pink crystals will point to areas where others may be helped; blue crystals suggest that the questioner seek expert advice. Arguments between friends can also show up here, especially when black or red crystals are present. Any crystal can indicate travel.

Key words: Service, adviser, travel, friends, disagreements

NORTH

The north deals with the integration of various threads of an issue to reach a successful conclusion. Crystals falling here will indicate the fruits of hard work. Certain crystals can hint at personal tendencies that may inhibit success unless watched. Yellow and blue crystals indicate the need to share knowledge.

Key words: Career, wisdom, going with the flow, security, perceived weakness

NORTHEAST

Crystals landing here pinpoint what is needed to improve a situation; the specific crystals will indicate what needs to be done. For example, yellow or clear stones show that more information is needed. Crystals that land here can also help to answer questions regarding love or illness.

Key words: Education, self-development, stillness, respite

EAST

All familial issues are anchored here. Green and red crystals indicate the need to respect other people's space; blue and yellow stones show a need to communicate. Black, red, and clear stones hint at issues that need attention. Violet and pink crystals suggest health concerns.

Key words: Family, relationships, responsibility, health, personal boundaries

SOUTHEAST

If the question concerns money, this is the area to watch. Yellow and green crystals represent an added bonus, even if the overall reading appears negative. That which is needed to feel wealthy, be it money, health, or love, is likely to be shown here.

Key words: Wealth, prosperity, harmony

INTERPRETING THE ASTROLOGICAL BOARD

As with the Compass board, beginner casters are best off reading the crystals in the sequence that appears below, starting from the 1st house and ending with the 12th house. This systematic approach will help prevent confusion.

See page 39 for the meaning of crystals that fall in the following ways:

- outside the boundaries of the board or partly in
- on lines between directions or houses
- touching each other in the same or different sections
- at the center of the board
- touching your personal stone
- pointing in a certain direction
- in groups

See also pages 44-135 for interpretations of specific crystals cast upon the board.

1ST HOUSE
Crystals that land here will indicate first impressions of a situation. Any considerations that the questioner should examine will be highlighted here.
Key words: Appearances, individuality

2ND HOUSE
Issues surrounding money need to be closely examined. Black, clear, or red crystals can point to changes needed. Blue or green crystals here focus on truth and hint that motives and honesty are in question.
Key words: Money, possessions, values

3RD HOUSE
Crystals landing here relate to communication. Clear, yellow, or gold crystals indicate a need for precision. Black, brown, and red crystals show that confusion is creating difficulties. Family considerations are present if green crystals appear. Any crystal may signal travel.
Key words: Communication, family, gossip, travel

4TH HOUSE
The crystals that land here will clarify the situation at hand. Problems in the questioner's life can show up here. Look for situations that are fueling insecurity. Blue crystals suggest the need for independence. Orange, gold, or red crystals show that action is needed.
Key words: Home, roots, family, stability, protection

5TH HOUSE
Any crystal here suggests that more leisure time is needed. Green or blue crystals hint that more time should be spent outdoors. Pink, green, and red crystals indicate romance. Black crystals suggest undiscovered skills.
Key words: Creativity, romance, leisure

6TH HOUSE

This house deals with work and health matters. Clear or white crystals suggest that a readjustment of the situation at hand is needed to remedy matters. Violet crystals emphasize the healing facets of a question.

Key words: Work, healing, service, health issues, crisis points

7TH HOUSE

Crystals here suggest the existence of issues surrounding long-term relationships. Green crystals indicate a need to examine the balance of relationships. Black, clear, or red crystals hint at changing dynamics.

Key words: Relationships, partnerships

8TH HOUSE

This house can emphasize psychic input, especially if violet, dark blue, or black stones land here. The appearance of more than one crystal indicates that an event has been delayed. If the question involves money, green or gold crystals suggest the need for a decision.

Key words: Finance, endings, beginnings, subtle forces, deep emotions

9TH HOUSE

Crystal energies here are a means to extend existing knowledge into new areas. The appearance of more than one stone shows that the questioner's outlook is too narrow. Any crystal here can indicate travel. Blue and yellow crystals call attention to learning.

Key words: Education, travel, broadcasting, philosophy, expansion

10TH HOUSE

This house deals with the culmination of something—a career, a relationship, or a project. Crystals landing here show the factors affecting that outcome. They can also indicate how the questioner wants to be seen by others. Goals can also be shown here.

Key words: Career, ambition, status, planning

11TH HOUSE

The influence of friends is shown here. Blue crystals indicate the need to reassess what is really going on and to ascertain who is influencing the questioner. Pink crystals show the need to be more compassionate with acquaintances.

Key words: Friends, social life, group issues, ideals

12TH HOUSE

Interpretation of crystals here may be difficult. Red crystals suggest the need for action. All other crystals indicate areas that should be explored in the questioner's life. Most insights illuminated here involve areas of self-sabotage as a result of personal beliefs.

Key words: Introspection, silence, self-sabotage

SOUTHWEST

9th House

8th House

10th

The Crystals

The tools of divination have no intrinsic power in their own right; rather, their power derives from the meaning that is ascribed to them by the diviner. In the pages that follow, crystals are the tools of divination. The meanings given to each of the forty-five featured crystals are derived from their unique physical characteristics, historical uses, mythical attributes, and spiritual and healing properties, all of which are described for each crystal. Sample readings for the placement of each crystal on both the Compass and Astrological boards are also provided, to help you determine which energies are at play. The more you work with your crystals, the greater your sensitivity and intuition toward them will become.

Obsidian

Obsidian is found only in volcanic areas, where it forms from rapidly cooled lava. Born from the fire within the heart of the planet, obsidian can bring a strong sense of determination to conquer fear and face reality in a practical, grounded, and courageous way.

Obsidian

Color: black with white, gray, or red markings

Hardness: 6

Composition: glass (mix of silicates)

Qualities: grounding, purging, revealing

Main chakra: base

Obsidian is a noncrystalline glass, and contains small crystals of other minerals, especially quartz, feldspar, and iron. These tiny inclusions can create sparkling iridescence or colored patches in the opaque black rock. Snowflake obsidian has flecks of gray or white; mahogany obsidian has red-brown streaks; Apache Tears, found in the American southwest, are translucent brown-black pebbles of obsidian. Unpolished obsidian should always be handled with caution, as its edges can be very sharp.

MYTH AND HISTORY

Obsidian has been used to make razor-sharp arrowheads and knives since the Stone Age. In Central America, where there is a plentiful supply of obsidian, the Aztecs fashioned clubs, axes, and swords from the stone. It was also used in religious carvings and ornamental regalia.

In Europe during the Middle Ages, obsidian was a popular material with which to make spheres and magical mirrors for scrying (the art of seeing into the future or into other worlds). One well-known scryer was Dr. John Dee, adviser to Queen Elizabeth I of England, Royal Astrologer, diplomat, spy, and occultist. He used an obsidian scrying mirror to communicate with spirits and, working together with his assistant, Edward Kelley, he developed a system called "Enochian magic," which explores a multitude of spiritual realms ruled over by angelic beings.

SPIRITUAL AND HEALING PROPERTIES

As a stone that emerges with dramatic force from the depths of the Earth, obsidian is believed by many to bring hidden emotions to the surface. This makes it extremely useful in releasing long-held stresses and buried traumas. Like a volcanic eruption, this process may be a turbulent, unpleasant experience while it is going on, bringing old wounds, fears, and anxieties to the surface before they are released. Transformation always brings change, and change can sometimes be difficult to accept. Nevertheless, change is essential if we are to grow. Obsidian will release only outdated, unwanted remnants of our lives so that we can move forward, unencumbered by the past.

DIVINATORY INTERPRETATION

Obsidian has a clear relationship with Pluto, both the planetary body and the classical Greek god after which the planet was named. Pluto is the god of the underworld, keeper of hidden treasures.

Whenever obsidian appears in a reading, it is important to look for hidden factors that may be affecting your situation. Unexpected turns of events may be experienced, and any change will be neither slow nor easy. Fear may also be an issue that needs to be dealt with—either your own or other people's. Remember that fear usually arises when there is a feeling that events are beyond our control, or when we cannot see the whole picture. Fear can also appear when you are face to face with something that seems to be more powerful than you.

The nature of obsidian is both fiery and grounding. These qualities will see you through any obsidian-like eruptions, creating a conviction in your own fiery strength and an ability to stand equal to anyone on the planet.

SUGGESTED READINGS

Obsidian in center/First House
You may want to examine how you appear to others. Consider making changes in your appearance or your style of dress.

Obsidian in southeast/Second House
Deeply held beliefs or assumptions about money need to be reassessed before you can move forward.

Obsidian in east/Third House
Think before you speak. If you have strong opinions, wait a while and reconsider. Do you need to be more circumspect?

Obsidian in north/Fourth House
Long-standing difficulties with your family need to be resolved once and for all.

Obsidian in west/Fifth House
The true power of your creative skills is not yet apparent. Examine what is stopping you from fully expressing yourself.

Obsidian in Sixth House
Try not to underestimate the courage it takes to make changes in the way you work. The longer necessary change is put off, the harder it will be.

Obsidian in southwest/Seventh House
Painful topics that you have been avoiding with partners need to be recognized and, where possible, brought to the surface so they can be cleared.

Obsidian in Eighth House
Financial dealings must be approached with total honesty and openness, to avoid creating complications later.

Obsidian in northeast/Ninth House
Keep a watchful eye out for books or courses that will help you to unlock any talents that have thus far been unable to surface through lack of opportunity.

Obsidian in south/Tenth House
Reluctance to alter some aspect of your career may result in a loss of status in the eyes of those who you are trying to impress.

Obsidian in northwest/Eleventh House
Look for possible hidden jealousy from acquaintances. It could upset your current plans—unless dealt with carefully.

Obsidian in Twelfth House
Look to your dreams and daydreams for guidance in your daily life. They will confirm that you already know what you require and what needs to be done.

Base (root) chakra
Base of spine (perineum)

▲ *Crystals are placed on the base chakra.*

◄ *Powerful forces can be either constructive or destructive. If they are ignored or not taken into consideration, problems are much more likely to arise.*

Personality

The typical obsidian person is emotionally volatile and secretive, and is very good at uncovering hidden objects and information.

Energy

Transmuting, deep, hidden.

S c h o r l
(b l a c k   t o u r m a l i n e)

Schorl brings the strength and stability of the planet Earth into the human aura.

Schorl

Color: black, opaque, or slightly translucent

Hardness: 7.5

Composition: Na $(Mg,Fe,Li,Mn,Al)_3 Al_6(BO_3) Si_6 O_{18} (OHF)_4$ (complex borosilicate)

Qualities: protective, structuring, grounding

Main chakra: base

▲ *Tourmaline can help realign the structural aspects of the body, such as the bones and the muscles. Pulls and strains are often eased with the help of this crystal.*
► *The Earth's energy field varies from place to place. Tourmaline helps us adjust to these changes when we are traveling.*

Tourmaline is formed deep in fractures of the Earth's crust, along with minerals such as quartz, mica, and feldspar. It forms long, thin, three-sided crystals with parallel striations along the length of the prism. Schorl, the black variety, is the most common. Tourmaline is unusual in that, when it is heated, one end of the crystal becomes charged electrically positive, while the other end has a negative charge. This makes it useful as a switching device in many types of machinery.

MYTH AND HISTORY

The Ancient Greeks and Romans are known to have turned the colored varieties of tourmaline into magical gemstones. During the Middle Ages, tourmaline was not identified as a distinct mineral, as it so closely resembled the color of other gemstones. Later, Dutch traders visiting Ceylon (present-day Sri Lanka) came across tourmaline, then called *turmali* (meaning many-colored), and introduced it as a gemstone into eighteenth-century Europe.

SPIRITUAL AND HEALING PROPERTIES

Schorl is one of the best stones to use for protection from all sorts of negativity. The stone will deflect, rather than absorb, energy that is unbalancing, creating a safe, neutral space around itself.

This crystal can also bring consciousness back into the physical body very rapidly. It is deeply grounding, and can be used to restore normal awareness after healing or spiritual practices.

One of schorl's main features is that it is a stone of alignment; it will help the body to make physical readjustments if the bones and muscles are out of place due to injury or strain. It can also align the human body to the energies of planet Earth itself. This makes it a useful stone to carry when traveling around the world or moving somewhere new, as it helps to harmonize personal with planetary energy and reduces the effects of jetlag.

DIVINATORY INTERPRETATION

Schorl indicates a need to be in harmony with your surroundings. Without harmony, there may be some danger of encountering negativity on some level—or of simply being clumsy. Either can be avoided by making sure you are fully grounded, focused, and practical in your outlook.

This crystal suggests that the structure of things—the hidden foundations—need to be taken into account. Make sure that the basis of all your actions and relationships is secure and firm.

SUGGESTED READINGS

Schorl in center/First House
You have a need to be seen by others as practical and reliable.

Schorl in southeast/Second House
Be careful with your money. Don't purchase unnecessary items.

Schorl in east/Third House
Any communications need to be in harmony with those around you.

Schorl in north/Fourth House
Remember that your roots and home are your foundation. Begin from there.

Schorl in west/Fifth House
Focus your creative skills a little more. This placement is ideal for a new romance.

Schorl in Sixth House
Take extra care with your back when lifting or moving things.

Schorl in southwest/Seventh House
Keep the peace with those you love.

Schorl in Eighth House
Arguments with others may have upset you more than you thought.

Schorl in northeast/Ninth House
Keep your feet firmly on the ground when opportunities come your way.

Schorl in south/Tenth House
Time to consolidate your plans for the future in practical and realistic ways.

Schorl in northwest/Eleventh House
Make time to take walks in natural surroundings with appreciative friends.

Schorl in Twelfth House
Don't allow yourself to get carried away with impractical ideas or vague dreams.

Base (root) chakra
Base of spine (perineum)

▲ *Crystals are placed on the base chakra.*

Personality

Black tourmaline can represent people who are down-to-earth, practical, and at home wherever they are. These people may thrive in and seek out unusual or dangerous situations.

Energy

Protective, balancing.

Smoky Quartz

Smoky quartz is a stone of quietness. It contains within its hidden interior the seeds of change and of new beginnings, and the potential for creativity.

Smoky quartz has a characteristic smoky brown or gray transparency. The depth of color can be slight or almost black, and is caused when clear quartz has been exposed to natural sources of radiation—either from within the Earth or from ultraviolet wavelengths. Occasionally, manganese impurities are present. Smoky quartz is usually found in mountainous areas.

Smoky Quartz

Color: yellow-brown to black

Hardness: 7

Composition: SiO_2 (silicon dioxide)

Qualities: quieting, grounding, protecting

Main chakra: base

▶ *Like many minerals, smoky quartz is found in mountainous areas of the world. Erosion by wind, water, and frost gradually uncovers crystal-filled cavities in the rock.*

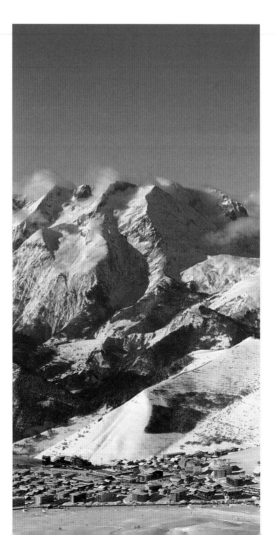

MYTH AND HISTORY

The Romans were well-aquainted with this stone; the dark, almost opaque black variety is called "morion" after the Latin name for it. A golden-brown variety of smoky quartz is found in Scotland, and is called "cairngorm" after the name of the mountain range in which it is found. Traditionally, fine examples of smoky quartz were polished and set as jewelry, and were handed down from generation to generation within a family as a protective or healing amulet.

SPIRITUAL AND HEALING PROPERTIES

Smoky quartz has a gentle focusing and grounding energy. Whereas clear quartz enlivens and radiates light energy, smoky quartz absorbs and stores all energy. This type of quartz is useful in any situation where there is confusion or overactivity. It energizes the grounding functions of the base chakra, so that the individual can focus on what is important. Smoky quartz also has a calming effect on the thought processes, and is an excellent stone for meditation. It can help to disperse fear and other negative states of mind and, because it creates stability in all body systems, it can provide security and protection.

▲ Smoky quartz encourages the mind to become still and contemplative. New ideas and solutions can suddenly cross the quiet mind.

DIVINATORY INTERPRETATION

Smoky quartz represents a stage of development where there is stillness. This can be right at the start, or even before the process of coming into being occurs. This stone is like the rich soil in which many things are able to grow when the time is right. In this context, it counsels patience and a very cautious level of activity, so as not to disturb the seeds of potential from sprouting.

At many stages of growth and development there are periods of quiescence, when nothing appears to be happening. Times like this indicate that change is under way at deep levels—probably well out of sight of everyday scrutiny. It is time to focus inwardly on plans and dreams, but do not settle or become fixed on any one outcome. Quiet contemplation, meditation, and withdrawal from outer activity can hasten the process.

SUGGESTED READINGS

Smoky Quartz in center/First House
Clarity is needed in the way in which a situation or person is being portrayed.

Smoky Quartz in southeast/Second House
Reexamine your thoughts on projects that have not yet begun. Do they need changing?

Smoky Quartz in east/Third House
It may be better to remain quiet or restrained.

Smoky Quartz in north/Fourth House
Spend time at home thinking about the entire situation.

Smoky Quartz in west/Fifth House
Focus on how you are actually going to begin or initiate plans.

Smoky Quartz in Sixth House
Changes may be needed in the way you work.

Base (root) chakra
Base of spine (perineum)

▲ Crystals are placed on the base chakra.

Smoky Quartz in southwest/Seventh House
Adjustments in relationships are likely.

Smoky Quartz in Eighth House
It is time to withdraw and reassess where deep feelings or commitments are taking you.

Smoky Quartz in northeast/Ninth House
More is happening than is apparent on the outside.

Smoky Quartz in south/Tenth House
It is time to examine your dreams closely. How can you make them a reality?

Smoky Quartz in northwest/Eleventh House
Now might be the time to avoid crowds and parties. You need some quiet time.

Twelfth House
Make sure that you have not overlooked any possibilities suggested by your dreams.

Personality

Smoky quartz people have a strong, quiet energy, and a deep, creative energy as well. Such a person may choose to lead a quiet life.

Energy

Potential, beginnings, change.

Rutilated Quartz

as "hair of Venus" or "arrows of love." The fine golden threads bear an uncanny resemblance to locks of golden hair, which appear to be trapped forever in the crystal.

Rutilated quartz is a combination of rock crystal intergrown with crystals of titanium dioxide called rutile.

Rutilated quartz

Color: transparent or smoky, with gold or brown inclusions

Hardness: 6–6.5

Composition: $SiO_2 + TiO_2$ (silicon dioxide with titanium dioxide)

Qualities: energizing, regenerating

Main chakras: all

▲▶ *One of the most striking varieties of quartz, rutilated quartz resembles blades of grass or hair trapped in crystal.*

In the modern world, rutile is a valuable material. Its titanium content is used to make a corrosion- and heat-resistant ore for use in the steel industry, as well as light, strong alloys for constructing aircraft. Rutile forms long, thin, needlelike crystals of golden-brown or red-brown, and is a common inclusion in quartz veins.

MYTH AND HISTORY

Rutilated quartz is well known in the Alps, where clear quartz can be found shot through with fine golden threads. Also known as sagenite or saginitic quartz, rutilated quartz was once a popular gemstone for a fashion of rings and necklaces known

▶ *All of the electrically controlled systems of the body benefit from the infusion of energy that rutilated quartz brings.*

SPIRITUAL AND HEALING PROPERTIES

Rutilated quartz can be of great benefit to damaged tissue. The interwoven and crossed patterns of rutile within the quartz stimulate the repair of wounds by encouraging a multilevel flow of energy. The stone can also be effective at restoring normal energy to over- or underactive areas of the body, the thin golden needles of rutile resembling the complex interdependence and communication among the systems of the body. The nervous system and all brain functions are also stimulated by rutilated quartz.

DIVINATORY INTERPRETATION

Rutilated quartz can show a complex, busy situation where it is necessary to understand and combine many different activities in order to get what you want. In a positive placement, rutilated quartz shows that circumstances are coming together, and that all the energies in a situation are beginning to pull in the same direction. Previously puzzling factors start to make sense, pieces fit into place, and a new coherence emerges.

In a negative placement, this stone may show a failure to integrate all the strands in your life and point them in a uniform direction. This state of affairs can indicate confusion or frustration, with too much going on at once. In these situations, rutilated quartz teaches that it is necessary to focus on the beauty of the whole, rather than trying to isolate and follow each single thread.

In certain placements, this stone may indicate that groups should pull together, or that the individual needs to seek the help of others.

SUGGESTED READINGS

Rutilated quartz in center/First House
An appearance of being focused on the issue or situation will help.

Rutilated quartz in southeast/Second House
Personal finances need to be consolidated and simplified.

Rutilated quartz in east/Third House
Confusing communications are creating problems—find out the truth.

Rutilated quartz in north/Fourth House
Get together with family or close friends for additional security.

Rutilated quartz in west/Fifth House
This is not a good time to take risks or follow whims. Act only when you are confident of the outcome.

Rutilated quartz in Sixth House
Busy times with lots of loose ends can create dissatisfaction. Relax into the situation.

Rutilated quartz in southwest/Seventh House
In the context of relationships, look at the partnership as a whole and not at current frustrations.

Rutilated quartz in Eighth House
Too many demands on your time and money are causing confusion and lack of energy.

Rutilated quartz in northeast/Ninth House
Reduce the distractions of too many ideas and opportunities before making any decisions.

Rutilated quartz in south/Tenth House
This is the right time to consolidate your present position. Pull in others for support where necessary.

Rutilated quartz in northwest/Eleventh House
Working as a group will help you achieve what you cannot manage alone.

Rutilated quartz in Twelfth House
Scattered thoughts and ideas need to be channeled into a single direction.

Crown chakra
Top of the head

Brow chakra
Center of forehead

Throat chakra
Neck

Heart chakra
Center of breastbone in center of chest

Solar plexus chakra
Midway between navel and base of ribs

Sacral chakra
Midway between navel and pubic bone

Base (root) chakra
Base of spine (perineum)

▲ Crystals are placed on all of the chakras.

Personality

The rutilated quartz personality has many irons in the fire, and is always busy with different ideas or projects. Poets, inventors, healers, group coordinators, and facilitators fit this stone's energy signature.

Energy

Consolidating, able to work with others.

Topaz

Topaz is a very valuable mineral that has been used in jewelry for thousands of years. The most prized varieties are imperial topaz—a rich orange color—and sherry topaz—a pale yellow color. Blue topaz bears a strong resemblance to aquamarine.

Topaz

Color: golden yellow, pink, blue, clear

Hardness: 8

Composition: $Al_2F_2SiO_4$ (aluminum fluorosilicate)

Qualities: energy balancing, stabilizing

Main chakra: solar plexus

▲ ▶ *In the Ayurvedic tradition, topaz comes under the influence of the planet and god Jupiter. Also known as Brihaspati, this deity is the teacher of the gods themselves.*
▶ ▶ *The falcon embodies clarity and power, thus making it a fitting image for engraving upon a topaz gemstone.*

Clear topaz is the most common topaz variety, and has the brilliance of diamond. Color in this stone is caused by small amounts of various metals in the atomic lattice. Crystals are usually four-sided columns with pyramidal or flat endings. One characteristic of topaz is the vertical striations along the prism faces.

Topaz is sensitive to heat, which will often change the color of the stone. It is hard but brittle, and can fracture easily. Although popular as a gemstone, topaz is less exclusive than other crystals due to its abundance.

MYTH AND HISTORY

"The figure of a falcon, if on a topaz, helps to acquire the goodwill of kings, princes, and magnates," says a thirteenth-century mystical treatise on gemstone designs.

Some believe the name "topaz" derives from the old name Topazos (now called Zebirgit), an island in the Red Sea on which the Romans discovered a fine source of yellow-green olivine, to which they gave the name *topazus*. They also used this name for many other yellow gemstones. In fact, old legends which speak of topaz may actually be referring to other yellow gemstones, such as yellow beryl or sapphire, as only recently have instruments been available to distinguish between these stones. Others believe that the name topaz derives from the Sanskrit word *tapas*, meaning fire or heat. Topaz is one of the most important of the nine gemstones of Ayurveda, representing the planet Jupiter.

SPIRITUAL AND HEALING PROPERTIES

Topaz is useful for directing and focusing energy; the stone's parallel striations and natural brilliance help this process. It also cleanses negativity from the emotions, bringing stability and balance. The energies within the self are better organized, creating confidence. The solar-plexus chakra—which relates to the maintenance of personal energy levels—is also stimulated by this gemstone. Yellow and golden topaz works well with the crown chakra, increasing peace and harmony, whereas the blue variety can release blockages of communication and expression.

DIVINATORY INTERPRETATION

In a reading, topaz encourages personal power and leadership. In a positive placement, it can show that now is the time to take the lead, and to gather others around you who can help you in your situation. In this scenario, it is important not to try to do everything yourself—learn to delegate and to trust the qualifications of others. A leader also needs to learn the most effective ways of encouraging others to want to follow his or her suggestions.

In a negative position, topaz suggests that you shouldn't be so domineering and bossy. Give those around you more space. Perhaps you expect to be the center of attention a little too often. Be aware that other people have needs and priorities too, and that you may not be included in these all of the time.

Topaz teaches us to watch how our energy moves out into the world. Are we being too selfish, narrow-minded, or demanding? Are we relying too much on others, fearful of our own ability to take control of the events that are occurring in our lives?

SUGGESTED READINGS

Topaz in center/First House
Be aware that you may appear to be demanding and authoritative to others.

Topaz in southeast/Second House
You need to take charge of your own resources and use them for your own needs.

Topaz in east/Third House
Don't be surprised if others ignore your advice—or if you wind up ignoring theirs.

Topaz in north/Fourth House
Recognize other people's needs when they are visiting you in your home, especially if you want them to stay.

Topaz in west/Fifth House
Your creative skills must be seen to be appreciated. Find ways of expressing them.

Topaz in Sixth House
You work well on your own, but don't be too proud to ask for help if you need it.

Topaz in southwest/Seventh House
Your dominant role in relationships can eclipse your partners' needs and abilities.

Topaz in Eighth House
Don't be pushed around by those who think that they know best, but do listen to what they have to say.

Topaz in northeast/Ninth House
The depth of your knowledge is evident, so don't be boastful when telling others.

Topaz in south/Tenth House
Go for it! This is the ideal time to do what you want and go where you want.

Topaz in northwest/Eleventh House
Social gatherings are a must at this time. Allow others to play a part in the planning and preparation.

Topaz in Twelfth House
Recharge your batteries in situations where someone else is providing you with your practical needs.

Solar plexus chakra
Midway between
navel and base of ribs

▲ *Crystals are placed on the solar plexus chakra.*

Personality

Topaz has a self-assurance that can be supportive or annoying, depending on how the personality is displayed. A natural leader or a manipulative schemer, this person will always find his or her way into top positions.

Energy

Regal, leader, delegator.

Bloodstone

Bloodstone is also known as heliotrope, and has a long tradition of magical use. A variety of chalcedony quartz, it has long been a valuable gemstone because of its striking red and green coloration.

Bloodstone

Color: green with
red speckles

Hardness: 7

Composition: SiO$_2$ (quartz)

Qualities: circulating,
supportive, motivating

Main chakras: heart, base

▲ *Because of its dynamic energy, bloodstone is associated with the astrological sign Aries. Both are ruled by the planet Mars.*

Bloodstone has the same chemical composition as green jasper, and is colored by small crystals of actinolite and celedonite. The red spots, which resemble blood, are iron oxide. The most valuable bloodstone has distinct bright red patterns and comes from India, which has always been its primary source.

MYTH AND HISTORY

A thirteenth-century mystical text states that "A bat, represented on heliotrope or bloodstone, gives the wearer power over demons and helps incantations."

There were many ancient beliefs revolving around bloodstone, or heliotrope (meaning "turning toward the sun"), as it was called in ancient times. Various texts suggested that it could turn water red, darken the sun, or summon storms. It was also thought to have the power to stop the flow of blood from wounds and to confer strength, longevity, and honor to its wearer.

▲ *Warriors would often carry bloodstone into battle to prevent blood loss if injured.*

SPIRITUAL AND HEALING PROPERTIES

The combined colors of bloodstone allow it to function at the levels of the base and heart chakras. It encourages a balance of energy; practicality, with the desire to grow; calming, strong emotions; and is both stimulating and motivating. The heart and circulation is supported at a physical, energetic level. Spiritual qualities can be accessed and integrated into everyday life because the base chakra, the source of our life force, is activated in a controlled and disciplined way.

DIVINATORY INTERPRETATION

Bloodstone is connected to the sun and to the astrological sign Aries. This connection, along with its relation to the blood, links it to the qualities of strength, courage, and the energy to succeed against all odds.

In a reading, bloodstone suggests the need for perseverance and courage, but also implies that it is indeed possible to achieve your goals. In a difficult placement, bloodstone offers some protection from defeat. In a positive position, it can show that all obstacles will come to nothing, and that those around you will support you.

In situations of emotional turbulence, the presence of bloodstone may indicate the need to calm impulsive reactions, such as anger. Don't allow your heart to let you get carried away from reality.

▼ *Bloodstone has long been connected to the sun, as both are able to harness the power of life energy to create new possibilities in the world.*

SUGGESTED READINGS

Bloodstone in center/First House
You need to be seen to be making a practical effort within the situation.

Bloodstone in southeast/Second House
Consider carefully any personal expenditure, financial or energetic, before you act.

Bloodstone in east/Third House
Constructive ideas and suggestions can be very supportive.

Bloodstone in north/Fourth House
Your loyalty and support may be needed by family or close friends.

Bloodstone in west/Fifth House
New romance or projects that have been slow to start will blossom now.

Bloodstone in Sixth House
Courage is needed to break out into new areas and to start again.

Bloodstone in southwest/Seventh House
Rethink your motives if others get angry with you—are you manipulating them?

Bloodstone in Eighth House
Careful investment will pay off, but you need to be patient.

Bloodstone in northeast/Ninth House
Plans to broaden your experience can be made now, step by step.

Bloodstone in south/Tenth House
You need to appreciate the fact that success comes from planning and hard work.

Bloodstone in northwest/Eleventh House
Enthusiasm for group work will be strong but short-lived—unless you can gain from it.

Bloodstone in Twelfth House
Enforced periods of solitude or rest are likely needed to prevent exhaustion.

Heart chakra
Center of breastbone in center of chest

Base (root) Chakra
Base of spine (perineum)

▲ *Crystals are placed on the heart and base chakras.*

Personality

This stone represents a courageous, strong individual. This person is emotional, but is able to balance passion with calmness and understanding.

Energy

Courageous, strong, supportive.

Emerald

Emerald is the quintessential green stone, yet it is rarely found free of faults or inclusions.

Emerald

Color: vivid green

Hardness: 7.5–8

Composition: $Be_3Al_2Si_6O_{18}$ (beryl, beryllium aluminum silicate)

Qualities: harmonious, cleansing, calming

Main chakra: heart

▲ *Faultless, clear emerald makes exceptional jewelry which encapsulates the green hues of the natural world.*

Emerald is a rare variety of the mineral beryl, which forms in granite and pegmatite rocks, growing long, hexagonal prisms. Beryl crystals can grow extremely large— specimens that are several yards in length are not uncommon. The particular shade of green that makes beryl so sought after is caused by atoms of vanadium and chromium within the crystal lattice.

Emerald is a hard but brittle mineral, and commonly contains fractures, gas bubbles, droplets of water, and crystals of other minerals. In fact, emerald can be easily identified from these inclusions. Mica inclusions are common in African and Russian stones, and calcite and pyrite inclusions often appear in Brazilian stones.

The finest gem-quality emeralds come mainly from Colombia. The highest-quality stones required by the gem trade are very expensive, but nontransparent emerald crystals with visible inclusions and fractures can often be acquired at a reasonable cost. The difficulty of finding perfect emeralds has led gem-cutters to devise a special "emerald cut," where a rectangular stone is given long facets on the outside edges to emphasize the color and disguise any imperfections.

MYTH AND HISTORY

The ancient Egyptians mined emeralds south of Koseir, in Egypt. The green color was associated with the life-giving properties of the River Nile and its surrounding vegetation. It became common practice to place an emerald in the mouth of a deceased person as they were mummified, so that they would spring up again in the afterlife. Green was the color sacred to Osiris (Asar), the guide and guardian of human beings, and the god of fertility, agriculture, and abundance. Thoth (Tahuti), the god of knowledge, is said to have imparted his wisdom upon an emerald tablet.

In South America, the Peruvians are said to have had an emerald the size of an ostrich's egg, which they kept in a special temple to the goddess of the stone, making offerings of smaller emeralds. Many large, fine emeralds were brought to Europe by the Spanish after they conquered the Aztecs.

Throughout history, emerald has been connected with honesty, truth, and holiness. These qualities made it the primary stone to consider when proving the strength and genuineness of a relationship. Thus, emerald became a stone representing true love. It has also been used to refresh or improve eyesight, protect from snakebites and evil spirits, and bring on the skills of prophecy and foresight. The stone was said to shatter in the vicinity of wickedness and deceit.

▲ Emerald was a symbol of life and knowledge to the ancient Egyptians.

SPIRITUAL AND HEALING PROPERTIES

Emerald brings soothing harmony to all systems of the body, and speeds all cleansing and purifying processes. It can release hidden fears and anxiety, allowing the individual to experience finer spiritual states of awareness. Emerald can thus be a useful meditation stone. The rich green color of the stone brings forth the energy of growth, peace, and abundance. The heart is the main area of balance for this stone.

DIVINATORY INTERPRETATION

Emerald in a reading indicates love, attachment, and true friendship. It requires an

honest and open approach. Like emerald itself, even the finest relationship has fractures and imperfections. A true partnership is stronger than these faults, but a superficial relationship will shatter when placed under pressure.

SUGGESTED READINGS

Emerald in center/First House
This stone shows the need to blend in and be at peace with your surroundings.

Emerald in southeast/Second House
Make sure that you truly appreciate and recognize what you have.

Emerald in east/Third House
Tell people you love how much you care, but don't expect them to reciprocate.

Emerald in north/Fourth House
"Home is where the heart is"—your sense of security stems from this adage.

Emerald in west/Fifth House
New romances and projects will benefit from your attention.

Emerald in Sixth House
You may need to consider changes at work if you don't really agree with what you are doing.

Emerald in southwest/Seventh House
Be loving with those in close relationships and open to everyone else.

Emerald in Eighth House
You have the skills to manage your own resources, if you trust yourself to do so.

Emerald in northeast/Ninth House
Share the wealth of your knowledge with those who care about the same issues.

Emerald in south/Tenth House
Pour your heart into the situation without expecting anything in return.

Emerald in northwest/Eleventh House
Friends are very important to you, as they can help you to keep your balance and perspective.

Emerald in Twelfth House
You need to be honest with yourself about your relationships regarding what you give and what you expect in return.

Heart chakra
Center of breastbone in center of chest

▲ *Crystals are placed on the heart chakra.*

Personality

An emerald personality is open, clear-sighted, and loving. There is a quiet, strong energy, a conviction of the rightness of things, and an optimism borne of confidence and stability rather than wishful thinking.

Energy

Loving, optimistic, friendly.

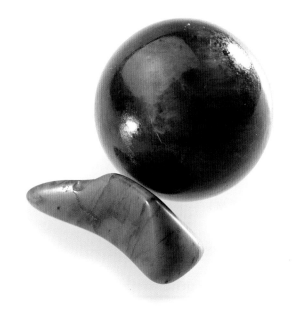

Jade

Although it is one of the hardest known minerals, jade— known also as jadeite and nephrite—has long been sought out as a stone for carving.

Jadeite

Color: green

Hardness: 7

Composition: $NaAlSi_2O_5$ (jadeite)

Qualities: integrating, instinctual, aware

Main chakra: heart

Nephrite

Color: green, white, cream, brown

Hardness: 6–6.5

Composition: $Ca(MgFe)_5Si_8O_{22}(OH)_2$ (nephrite)

Qualities: integrating, instinctual, aware

Main chakra: heart

▶ *Worn as jewelry, jade can improve the efficiency of all healing processes.*

The name jade actually refers to two distinct minerals: jadeite and nephrite. Jadeite is slightly harder and has a deep-green coloring from impurities of chromium, whereas nephrite is softer and less dense.

As high-quality jade is uncommon, imitations are frequent; bowenite, a similar mineral to serpentine, is often stained green to imitate the rich color of Imperial jade, while African jade is actually opaque green garnet, from the Transvaal region.

MYTH AND HISTORY

Jade has a long and distinguished history, beginning at the dawn of civilization. Jade ax-heads of both ceremonial and ritual function have been found in Stone Age tombs. Some have been deliberately cut up or divided, suggesting a ritual of passing on the power of the deceased. In South America, jade was placed under the tongues of the dead. This practice was common in China, too, to protect the spirit of the deceased.

The widespread use of jade in America was noted by the Spanish invaders, who brought many pieces back to Europe. They named the stone *piedra de hijada*, meaning "stone of the flank," because the Native Americans used it to treat kidney disease.

In China, jade was afforded the highest medicinal value. It was used to prolong life and strengthen the heart, lungs, voice, bones, and blood.

New Zealand is another important source of jade. The Maoris carved it into stylized human forms representing the ancestral spirits. Through these *hei-tiki*, meaning "carvings for the neck," the energy of the ancestors could be accessed by descendants' families.

SPIRITUAL AND HEALING PROPERTIES

Jade has an overall balancing effect on the heart. It is a stabilizing gemstone, as it helps bring awareness of the body's instinctual capacity. This level of awareness maintains a continual connection with the planet and its energies, creating a sense of belonging and an increased sensitivity to surroundings. Jade also improves the efficiency of all healing processes.

DIVINATORY INTERPRETATION

Jade provides an instinctive ability to sense the truth of any situation. In a reading, it may suggest that we should listen to our gut feelings more often. Jade's strength comes from its ability to connect the individual to the whole. It can therefore imply that we should either become more involved with a situation, or back off if our instincts tell us to do so.

As jade has a long relationship with the spirits of the dead, in a reading it can represent the traditions of our forebears. We are all connected to our ancestral genetic makeup, including its behavioral tendencies. Acknowledgment of this fact can provide insight into our personal lives.

SUGGESTED READINGS

Jade in center/First House
You have a need to appear to feel at home in any situation.

Jade in southeast/Second House
Trust yourself and follow your own beliefs and values.

Jade in east/Third House
It is a good idea to clarify how you feel and where you stand.

Jade in north/Fourth House
Inspiration can be found by looking at your family history.

Jade in west/Fifth House
You need to follow your own instincts when it comes to fun and enjoyment.

Jade in Sixth House
Continue to do things the way they have always been done.

Jade in southwest/Seventh House
Don't let your need to please others stop you from addressing your own needs.

Jade in Eighth House
When advice is given by those in authority, weigh it against your own gut reactions.

Jade in northeast/Ninth House
Make sure you know all the background history that has created the current situation.

Jade in south/Tenth House
Appreciate that where you are now is the result of many factors, not just your own efforts.

Jade in northwest/Eleventh House
Those who share the same roots as you can help you feel a sense of belonging.

Jade in Twelfth House
Examine any traditions that you follow or have adopted and make sure they fulfill your needs.

Heart chakra
Center of breastbone in center of chest

▲ *Crystals are placed on the heart chakra.*

Personality

Jade represents those who are rooted in the traditions of family. There is a stability in these people that comes from a sense of continuity.

Energy

Stable, belonging, ancestral.

Malachite

Malachite is a copper ore. It has also been called "rock green," "the velvet ore," and "the satin ore," because of its striking colors and patterns.

Malachite

Color: concentric bands of light and dark green

Hardness: 3.5–4

Composition: $Cu_2CO_3(OH)_2$ (carbonate of copper)

Qualities: detoxifying, soothing

Main chakra: heart

▶ *Universally, the evil eye describes a look inspired by jealousy or maliciousness. In the past, especially when used by a witch or an enemy, it was thought to have the power to cause ills of all sorts, including bad luck and disease—even death.*

Malachite is a soft mineral often found in combination with blue azurite. Both minerals are formed from the decomposition of copper ores exposed to water and air, making them good indicators of the presence of copper. Malachite rarely forms crystals, forming nodules instead that are a deep, silky green. Its concentric bands of color make it a valuable decorative stone, despite its softness.

MYTH AND HISTORY

The name malachite derives from the Greek word for the mallow plant, *maloche*, the leaves of which are a similar shade of green.

Since classical times, malachite has been used as a protective amulet. Malachite carved with a sun's face was thought to provide protection from harm, evil spirits, and venomous animals. The concentric patterns of malachite often resemble an eye, and so, naturally, it was also used as a protection from the evil eye—the curse of a witch or an enemy. The ancient Egyptians mined the stone to use for decorative purposes and as a green pigment.

SPIRITUAL AND HEALING PROPERTIES

An absorbing stone, malachite is excellent for drawing out imbalances from the body. It has also been used to reduce the pain of inflammation, and can soothe minor aches and pains.

Malachite is particularly effective at clearing emotional imbalances, and can bring peace and balance to the heart chakra. It also helps cleanse the body of toxins and pollutants. Care should be taken with malachite, however, as its dust is toxic if ingested.

DIVINATORY INTERPRETATION

In a reading, malachite suggests that there are many emotional levels which need to be taken into consideration, and signals that perhaps more care should be taken when dealing with emotional issues. As well, this stone intimates that letting go of old patterns, memories, and attachments is now necessary. Growth and the ability to move forward are contingent upon the ability to forgive—if not to forget. Painful situations must be understood, forgiven, and sent on their way. To do otherwise is to become trapped in the past.

In many ancient cultures, the evil eye was a common form of curse brought about by malevolent thoughts toward a person through jealousy or some other negative emotion. Make sure that you are not guilty of wishing harm upon others, and take care that you are not suffering yourself from strong negative emotions directed at you from nearby. Harboring grudges and apportioning blame are life-damaging both to ourselves and to the person to whom the grudge and blame are directed.

Malachite teaches that there are many shades and levels to our actions. In a positive placement, it indicates a protected space, free from harm, in which it is possible to feel free and to grow.

SUGGESTED READINGS

Malachite in center/First House
Any jealousy or envy will be difficult to hide from others at the moment.

Malachite in southeast/Second House
Change your views as to why you think things are happening as they are.

Malachite in east/Third House
Take care that your immediate responses do not stem more from fear and anger than from logic.

Malachite in north/Fourth House
Older people's views may be at odds with your own. Allow them their opinions.

Malachite in west/Fifth House
Look for activities that you enjoy to reduce your stress levels.

Malachite in Sixth House
Don't ignore any health problems, particularly if they are inherited.

Malachite in southwest/Seventh House
Allow partners to soothe your fears and anxieties.

Malachite in Eighth House
Forgive the people who seem to be responsible and your pain will ease.

Malachite in northeast/Ninth House
Spread your wings and break away from the thought patterns that have trapped you for so long.

Malachite in south/Tenth House
If you feel thwarted in your ambitions, look to your own assumptions for the cause.

Malachite in northwest/Eleventh House
You may need to develop your defenses, as other people see you as the reason for their own upsets.

Malachite in Twelfth House
This is not a good time to manipulate situations behind the scenes, as you are seeing only part of the picture.

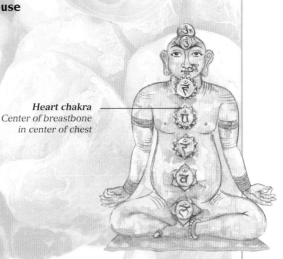

Heart chakra
Center of breastbone in center of chest

▲ *Crystals are placed on the heart chakra.*

◄ *The mallow plant, for which malachite is named, has the same properties as the stone: soothing and calming.*

Personality

A positive malachite person is a healing, soothing character who will always help to ease another's pain, and will offer support in times of emotional turmoil. A negative malachite person is resentful, controlling, and difficult to trust.

Energy

Soothing, pain-relieving, calming.

Moldavite

Moldavite is a unique gemstone created by the explosive impact of meteorites millions of years ago.

Moldavite

Color: glassy, bright green

Hardness: 5

Composition: amorphous silicates (glass)

Qualities: perceptive, intuitive

Main chakras: heart, throat, brow, crown

Moldavite is the only gem-quality member of a small group of mysterious minerals known as tektites. Tektites are found throughout the world, and are thought to result from the massive heat and pressure waves generated by meteorite strikes on or close to the surface of the planet. They are glassy in composition, but have none of the trace elements expected from volcanic material. Most take the form of extruded drops, pebbles, and splatter shapes.

All tektites are opaque and earth-colored with the exception of moldavites, which are found only in a small area of the Czech Republic, where they were formed some 15 million years ago. Deep, rich-green moldavites have been dug from sandpits, collected from fields, and used as ornaments and amulets for centuries. Most are small, with rippled and cratered surfaces.

MYTH AND HISTORY

This stone has been known to exist in central Europe for a long time, but it is only in the last couple of decades that any significant amounts have been made available. Unlike that of other gemstones, the volume of moldavite is finite—no other sources have been discovered and, as the product of some distant and unique event, another source is unlikely.

Moldavite is sometimes called an extraterrestrial stone, or a green meteorite. Tests show this to be unlikely, but there is no real consensus as to how tektite actually came into being. Yet, those who have tuned into the energy of moldavite have been known to experience a series of strange, unearthly sensations, including speed, great heat, and a sense of expanded awareness.

◄ *A variety of tektites collected from sites in Texas, Vietnam, and Australia.*

SPIRITUAL AND HEALING PROPERTIES

Moldavite amplifies the qualities of any other stones nearby, emphasizing their spiritual aspects. On its own, it activates the spiritual qualities of the heart chakra, particularly the relationship of the self to the universe and the quest for personal fulfillment. At the throat, brow, and crown chakras, moldavite enhances subtle perception, intuition, and visualization, and provides a fuller appreciation of existence.

DIVINATORY INTERPRETATION

Moldavite's power comes from the violent forces unleashed when outer and inner space meet. Similarly, sometimes a shock is needed to make us realize that we have been living in a self-constructed dream of reality rather than in reality itself. Moldavite may indicate an awakening experience of any kind—not just one that is explosive. In either case, however, the result will be the same: a sudden broadening of experience and perception that changes our relationship to everything that is familiar. This may be difficult to deal with, or it may result in a natural feeling of opening up to new worlds.

The presence of moldavite in a reading can also indicate a sudden and unexpected turn of events that can be the beginning of a great opportunity—assuming change is allowed to happen.

◀ *The mysterious nature of moldavite has linked it to several powerful mystical objects, including the Holy Grail.*

SUGGESTED READINGS

Moldavite in center/First House
Others are likely to misunderstand or misread your intentions.

Moldavite in southeast/Second House
Sudden changes in personal finances or situations are possible at this time.

Moldavite in east/Third House
You need to speak up, even if it seems out of place and is out of character.

Moldavite in north/Fourth House
Upsets in the home are likely, but they are for the best in the long run.

Moldavite in west/Fifth House
Allow your sense of wonder to re-awaken—spend some time in natural surroundings.

Moldavite in Sixth House
Unexpected shifts in—and your attitude toward—the way you work may open up new possibilities.

Moldavite in southwest/Seventh House
All relationships have their ups and downs. Don't take these fluctuations personally.

Moldavite in Eighth House
Open your eyes to the wider events going on in the world and how these control our lives.

Moldavite in northeast/Ninth House
Be open to all possibilities and probabilities—the sky is the limit.

Moldavite in south/Tenth House
Be prepared to stand out from the crowd and be labeled as such—for better or worse.

Moldavite in northwest/Eleventh House
Look closely at information concerning ecology, nature, and the environment for inspiration or guidance.

Moldavite in Twelfth House
Take time out to connect or reconnect with the Earth. This will help you to put everything into perspective.

Crown chakra
Top of the head

Brow chakra
Center of forehead

Throat chakra
Neck

Heart chakra
Center of breastbone in center of chest

▲ *Crystals are placed on the crown, brow, throat, and heart chakras.*

Personality

The moldavite personality is strong and unconventional, and may have atypical or unpopular views. Big ideas and the desire to push the limits of experience are also characteristic.

Energy

Universal, expansive aware, awakened.

Moss Agate

Of all the wonderful variety within agate, moss agate is the most fascinating for its resemblance to the forms of living plants.

Moss agate

Color: clear quartz with green and brown inclusions

Hardness: 6.5

Composition: SiO_2

Qualities: open, cleansing, optimistic

Main chakra: heart

▲▶ *A wonderful vehicle for attuning to the earth, moss agate is a particularly useful stone for gardeners.*

Moss agate is transparent or translucent chalcedony quartz that has intergrown with crystals of manganese oxides, hornblende, and sometimes oxides of iron. These inclusions are usually green and brown, and take a dendritic form—that is, they resemble plant forms in the way they grow.

MYTH AND HISTORY

Moss agate was once known as "mocha stone," after one of the main sources of the mineral, the town of Al Mukna (Mocha) on the Red Sea coast of Yemen. It has long been sought for ornamental uses such as cameo brooches, rings, and vases.

SPIRITUAL AND HEALING PROPERTIES

The green coloring within moss agate naturally aligns its energy with the heart chakra.

The treelike patterns are also reminiscent of the fine airways of the lungs and the small capillary blood vessels, as well as the channels of the lymphatic system. Where there is congestion and constriction in the lungs, blood, or lymph supplies, moss agate will help to free up those passageways. It can also be useful for detoxification processes.

Moss agate encourages openness within the mind and emotions, creating feelings of expansion, freedom, and space. These feelings create confidence and the desire to experience new things in life.

Due to its natural-looking shapes and predominant colors, moss agate resonates with all realms of nature. It also encourages awareness of the natural world and helps plant growth.

DIVINATORY INTERPRETATION

Moss agate brings the spirit of the natural world into a reading, and may suggest that spending more time enjoying the open spaces and green silence of the countryside would be beneficial. Because an escape to the countryside is a well-known antidote to overwork, tension, and other constricting circumstances of an urban lifestyle, the appearance of this stone may imply that stress is a current problem in the questioner's life. This stress may stem from a sense of duty or obligation; a difficult and demanding job; emotional or relationship problems causing insecurity or indecision; or feelings of being trapped. In order to come to terms with these restrictions, space and balance of mind are required.

In our lives, we are usually offered a choice of paths down which to travel; this stone suggests that the time has come to choose a path and move along it. Even a short distance away, a problem can cease to look like an insurmountable obstacle. Whatever the problem, moss agate implies that it's time to gain some perspective.

◀ The many treelike, branching structures within the human body all respond well to the presence of moss agate, which helps to relieve constriction and blockages.

SUGGESTED READINGS

Moss agate in center/First House
You need to make a new start, to find space, and to be yourself.

Moss agate in southeast/Second House
Look for new ways to get what you have always wanted.

Moss agate in east/Third House
It is time to listen to what people are really saying rather than what you think they are saying.

Moss agate in north/Fourth House
Personal space is paramount now. Certain steps are required to insure you get it.

Moss agate in west/Fifth House
Time spent outdoors will help rekindle your enjoyment of life.

Moss agate in Sixth House
You need to make changes to your work environment so that you feel more comfortable.

Moss agate in southwest/Seventh House
Say what is in your heart. Share your feelings.

Moss agate in Eighth House
Restrictions imposed by society may be obstructing your choices.

Moss agate in northeast/Ninth House
Choices on offer are not binding forever. Opportunities will come again.

Moss agate in south/Tenth House
Look for ways to broaden your approach to your work and ambitions.

Moss agate in northwest/Eleventh House
Reach out to new friends and develop new areas of interest.

Moss agate in Twelfth House
Make time to be alone and reflect on your life. Choices and directions will be clarified this way.

Heart chakra
Center of breastbone in center of chest

▲ *Crystals are placed on the heart chakra.*

Personality

The moss agate person is a free spirit. He or she is at ease with nature, and is able to make do with whatever resources are available. This individual is a poet or dreamer, and can't stand to be pinned down or restricted by outside constraints.

Energy

Natural, curious, spacious.

Aventurine

It is thought that this variety of quartz, with its many colors and sparkling inclusions, derives its name from the Italian phrase per avventura, *meaning "chance."*

Aventurine

Color: green, orange-brown

Hardness: 7

Composition: SiO_2 with inclusions

Qualities: tranquil, positive

Main chakras: solar plexus, heart

◣▶ *The calming qualities of aventurine make it particularly suitable for both meditation and emotional healing.*
▶▶ *Aventurine can help provide clarity of direction, thus presenting the opportunity to discover new life paths.*

Aventurine forms when quartz melts and recrystallizes in the presence of other minerals that color the body of the rock. It is microcrystalline, and forms large slabs and masses, making it useful for creating ornamental objects.

Green aventurine is colored by fuschite mica, which gives the stone a sprinkling of bright speckles. Although often subtle, this feature distinguishes it from similar-looking stones such as amazonite, emerald, and jade. Brown varieties take their color from pyrites or goethite.

MYTH AND HISTORY

Aventurine has been valued by many civilizations over the centuries. Aventurine carvings from China date from the third century BC, and the stone was also used for carving in the Mediterranean area. Today aventurine remains a popular carving stone, particularly in India, China, and Brazil.

The origin of the present name for the stone may come from the Italian phrase *per avventura*, meaning "by chance" (thus implying that the discovery of the stone was accidental). It is also possible that the stone is named after a spangled type of decorative glass called avventura, which the stone resembles.

SPIRITUAL AND HEALING PROPERTIES

Green aventurine is perhaps the best balancing stone for the heart chakra. It encourages calmness and positivity, and helps to release emotional pain in a gentle, effective way. In any color, aventurine is both a cleanser of negativity and an activator of positive life-supporting qualities. It can help to release childhood anxieties and fears, and is useful in certain spiritual practices, including meditation and creative visualization. In traditional Tibetan healing practices, aventurine is used for improving eyesight as well as clarity of insight, perception, and creativity.

The golden-brown varieties of aventurine work best at the level of the solar plexus, bringing increased self-confidence and an optimistic outlook on life.

DIVINATORY INTERPRETATION

When aventurine appears in a reading, it indicates that new opportunities may arise. Like the shining sparkles in the stone itself, these will need to be looked for carefully, and are most likely to appear where you least expect them to be.

In a positive placement, aventurine offers the chance of freedom, a sudden new departure, or a new road along which to travel. In a difficult placement, aventurine may suggest that the questioner is oblivious to certain opportunities to improve the current situation that are presenting themselves. More attention must be paid to details, as these may lead to a breakthrough.

SUGGESTED READINGS

Aventurine in center/First House
Enthusiasm to explore the situation could get excessive and end up scattering your focus.

Aventurine in southeast/Second House
Prudence and care with money will help you to resist the temptation to overspend.

Aventurine in east/Third House
Freedom of speech is crucial if you are to maintain your right to choose for yourself.

Aventurine in north/Fourth House
By making adjustments at home, you will gain more space or freedom.

Aventurine in west/Fifth House
Don't overlook the small possibilities in the bigger picture.

Aventurine in Sixth House
If you feel trapped, make minor changes to relieve the strain until you can really act.

Aventurine in southwest/Seventh House
New people in your life need time to get to know you—and time is needed for you to trust them.

Aventurine in Eighth House
Examine everything closely so you are clear about where you stand.

Aventurine in northeast/Ninth House
Taking a risk is probably worthwhile, but be on the lookout for unseen factors.

Aventurine in south/Tenth House
New avenues or directions may surface. Be cautious before committing yourself.

Aventurine in northwest/Eleventh House
You may feel like leaving the crowd behind to do things by yourself.

Aventurine in Twelfth House
Changing the way you think can be the easiest way to go about creating new situations out in the world.

Heart chakra
Center of breastbone in center of chest

Solar plexus chakra
Midway between navel and base of ribs

▲ *Crystals are placed on the solar plexus and heart chakras.*

Personality

The personality represented by this stone is optimistic, bright, and emotionally balanced, with clear insight. Perhaps this person is a practitioner of meditation that uses visual imagery.

Energy

Opportunity, chance, freedom.

Carnelian

A stone of gentle healing, carnelian exudes a warmth that is both soothing and very powerful.

Carnelian

Color: red-orange

Hardness: 7

Composition: SiO_2 (silicon dioxide—chalcedony)

Qualities: healing, soothing, creative

Main chakra: sacral

▲ *An Egyptian carnelian seal ring from the 2nd millenium BC carved with the seals of Ramses II and Nefertiti.*
▶ *The ancient Egyptians saw carnelian, with all its creative energy, as the perfect stone upon which to carve extracts from* The Book of the Dead.

Carnelian is a variety of quartz known as chalcedony. Chalcedony forms in a different manner from rock crystal, in tightly packed layers or rounded aggregates of very fine fibers. It is the pores between these fibers that allow chalcedony to exist in such a variety of colors. Nearly all of these varities have been given distinct names— carnelian, jasper, chrysoprase, to name a few—and most have a history of decorative use.

Chalcedony crystallizes in pockets of rock where silica-rich gel collects. It also forms from the erosion of other minerals, such as serpentine.

MYTH AND HISTORY

Found in India, Arabia, and Egypt, carnelian was highly valued as a gemstone in ancient times, particularly the orange variety, known as "sard." It was used to carve early Babylonian cylinders for recording information and for official and personal seals. In ancient Egypt, carnelian was one of the main stones used to make amulets into which were carved extracts from *The Book of the Dead.* Carnelian is also one of the stones in the High Priest's breastplate mentioned in the *Book of Exodus,* verse 27. Here it is called *odem,* and is associated with the tribe of Reuben. In classical Greece and Rome, carnelian was one of the most popular materials for carving magical amulets .

Today, the finest carnelian, which has a red-orange color, comes from the vicinity of Bombay, India.

SPIRITUAL AND HEALING PROPERTIES

As a healing stone, carnelian is gently activating and warming, and will encourage the natural healing abilities of the body. This is partly because it energizes the sacral chakra, where stress and trauma tends to become lodged. Carnelian helps to gently

▲ *Like sunlight, carnelian brings a warm, soothing energy to the body, helping it to release stress and tension.*

release these imbalances, even if they have been present for many years. Orange is one of the best colors to use where shock, or an accident or illness have occurred. Where there is rigidity, stiffness, or inflammation, carnelian can help to restore the correct energy flow.

DIVINATORY INTERPRETATION

In a positive placement, carnelian indicates a great deal of creative energy. Love of life, happiness, enjoyment, and harmony with those around you are all suggested by this stone. Carnelian also represents the energy of movement and the flexibility of "going with the flow." It suggests that you should work with that which presents itself to you, rather than forging ahead in search of a distant goal. Both success and an increase in positive energies are favored by this stone.

In a difficult position, carnelian may warn that flexibility should be encouraged, or you may find yourself suffering from the negative associations of this stone, including stress, illness, inertia, and an inability to progress. Deep pain and old wounds may also need attention before they create further problems.

SUGGESTED READINGS

Carnelian in center/First House
Take events as they come. Don't let anything faze or upset you.

Carnelian in southeast/Second House
Now is the time to deal with old emotional pain that has recently surfaced.

Carnelian in east/Third House
Take care to insure that you are completely understood in your communications.

Carnelian in north/Fourth House
You need to take time out to relax at home or away from crowds of people.

Carnelian in west/Fifth House
Put aside time to just enjoy being alive, without the pressures of your world.

Carnelian in Sixth House
If you are having health problems, you may benefit from a visit to a healer.

Carnelian in southwest/Seventh House
Insure good communication so that harsh words or actions in partnerships are clarified and understood.

Carnelian in Eighth House
If financial deals or emotional ties are holding you back, consider releasing them for good.

Carnelian in northeast/Ninth House
Sharing your knowledge will help others to recover from past problems.

Carnelian in south/Tenth House
Creativity and adaptability are needed for success and its enjoyment.

Carnelian in northwest/Eleventh House
Time spent repairing friendships that have been recently bruised will help all concerned.

Carnelian in Twelfth House
Pay attention to personal requirements and look for ways to meet your needs.

Sacral chakra
Midway between navel and pubic bone

▲ *Crystals are placed on the sacral chakra.*

Personality

Carnelian represents a warm, friendly, caring, and sympathetic person who has experienced much in life. This person is also creative, nurturing, sensual, and sensitive.

Energy

Healing, creative, sympathetic.

Copper

*Copper, which forms natural nuggets and treelike shapes,
was the first metal to be worked by humankind.*

Copper

Color: orange-red with green
oxides, metallic

Hardness: 2.5–3

Composition:
Cu (elemental copper)

Qualities: harmonizing,
flowing, calming

Main chakras: base, sacral,
solar plexus, heart

Copper is formed from the alteration of
copper-bearing solutions and other minerals. Native copper, the natural crystals or
nuggets, is formed in zones where other
copper ores are located. Copper ores, which
are usually a strong green color, are very
common. The metal has a low melting
point and can be easily worked due to its
softness. Like most elemental metals,
copper is a good conductor of electricity,
and is in great demand for electrical wiring.

MYTH AND HISTORY

Copper's name derives from the Roman
words *Cyprium aes,* meaning "metal from
Cyprus," where the Romans found plentiful
supplies. Copper was the first metal to be
used by humankind simply because, unlike
most other metals, it was found in pure,
soft, workable nuggets.

About 8,000 years ago, copper was beat-
en into simple tools. At some point it
began to be melted, and was then added to
tin ore to make bronze, a much stronger
alloy. By about 4000 BC bronze had become
the main material for weapons, tools, and
ornaments. Later, copper became a major
source of wealth from trade, and created
important links among far-flung cultures.

▶ *In ancient Roman
mythology, copper was
associated magically with
Venus, both the planet
and the goddess. In
ancient Greek mythology,
Cyprus, where copper is
abundant, is said to be
the birthplace of the
goddess Aphrodite (the
Greek name for Venus),
whose name means
"of the foam."*

▶ *Copper bracelets are an effective way to reduce inflammation and pain. They can also help ease the effects of difficult planetary positions, such as emotional swings and mental upset.*

SPIRITUAL AND HEALING PROPERTIES

Copper is often used to reduce the pain and inflammation of arthritis and rheumatism. It is not only an excellent conductor of electricity, but it also helps the flow of many types of energy throughout the body. Nervous system and brain functions are strengthened, and there can be a release of frustration, tension, and nervous energy.

DIVINATORY INTERPRETATION

Copper will smooth and integrate all energies that are found around it. If there is potential for conflict, copper will ease the aggression. If there is resistance or a blockage preventing movement, copper will help the energy to flow constructively once more. It will also help all communications and improve emotional situations.

Copper reminds us to remain open to negotiation, to be willing to accept new input, and not to become irritated by the behavior of others.

SUGGESTED READINGS

Copper in center/First House
You need to show others that you can cope with anything and are willing to start again.

Copper in southeast/Second House
You may be creating your own difficulties by maintaining inappropriate or rigid views.

Copper in east/Third House
Keep all communication lines open and delay any decisions until you have all the information you need.

Copper in north/Fourth House
Insure that any emotional tension with family members is released before it has the chance to become established.

Copper in west/Fifth House
Leisure activities and romance may seem to be at a standstill at the moment. Have patience.

Copper in Sixth House
Consider taking advice from others with respect to health or work situations.

Copper in southwest/Seventh House
Seeing another person's viewpoint will avoid unnecessary conflict with those dear to you.

Copper in Eighth House
Delays in money matters could cause frustration. Just accept situations that you cannot alter.

Copper in northeast/Ninth House
Examine what may be stopping you from exploring matters further.

Copper in south/Tenth House
If you wish to get things moving, you must pay more attention to the situation.

Copper in northwest/Eleventh House
Friends and colleagues may need you to act as a diplomat to settle some disagreements.

Copper in Twelfth House
You need time alone to integrate and absorb all that is happening.

Heart chakra
Center of breastbone in center of chest

Solar plexus chakra
Midway between navel and base of ribs

Sacral chakra
Midway between navel and pubic bone

Base (root) chakra
Base of spine (perineum)

▲ *Crystals are placed on the heart, solar plexus, sacral, and base chakras.*

Personality

The copper person is a mediator, and is able to make positive suggestions in any situation. Creative, practical, and flexible, he or she may appear to be all things to all people.

Energy

Flexible, mediator, integrated.

◀ *The modern world is reliant upon copper for its ability to conduct electricity, bringing us power and enhancing our communications.*

Garnet

Garnet can spark into flame anything that comes into contact with its fiery nature.

Garnet

Color: red, brown, orange, green

Hardness: 6.5 –7.5

Composition: $X_3Y_2(SiO_4)_3$ where X and Y are various metals (silicates of bivalent and trivalent elements)

Qualities: energizing, accelerating

Main chakra: base

Garnet is formed at very high temperatures, from a complex mixture of minerals with similar compositions. Because of this method of formation, garnet has a wider range of color than any other stone, though the best known and most sought after are the red varieties. Garnets are often found as large granules or clusters within rock, and are roughly ball-shaped, with many facets. They are dense and break easily, though their sharp edges make them ideal as an abrasive material.

MYTH AND HISTORY

Ragiel's *Book of Wings*, a thirteenth-century mystical text, says that "The well-formed image of a lion, if engraved on a garnet, will protect and preserve honors and health, cure the wearer of all diseases, bring him honors, and guard him from all perils in traveling."

The name "garnet" is thought to derive from the Latin word *punica granatum*, meaning pomegranate, because of the resemblance of the seeds to the stone.

▲ *Where there is a need for energy, dynamism, and action, a deep red garnet stone will have an immediate stimulating effect.*

SPIRITUAL AND HEALING PROPERTIES

The particular color of a garnet specimen will determine its exact effect, but garnet will always work to focus and activate. Red garnets are the best energizing stones for the body, speeding up all processes and amplifying the effects of other stones placed nearby. All garnets are useful to get

▲ *Garnet derives its name from the pomegranate, whose seeds are bright red and occur in large numbers, just like garnet crystals in their rock matrix.*

things under way, although it is sometimes better to let other stones continue the work. Any cool, sluggish, watery conditions and states can be balanced by the energy of garnet, which introduces the fire element.

DIVINATORY INTERPRETATION

Garnet is an energizer and motivator; all dull, stagnant situations can be revitalized by its energy. It tends to amplify the strength of other stones—both their positive and difficult qualities—depending on the cast. Positively, garnet will stimulate and activate. Negatively, it will irritate and annoy. It can denote passion, but not necessarily of the long-lasting variety. It can show anger that flares up but quickly dies

down again, and can suggest new ideas or creativity that will fizzle out or become distracted if not balanced by other, more grounded, qualities. Like fire, garnet can sustain life and liveliness, or it can cause pain and burning.

SUGGESTED READINGS

Garnet in center/First House
Action is needed now, while energy is still available.

Garnet in southeast/Second House
This is not a good time to make decisions about long-term projects. Wait a few days.

Garnet in east/Third House
The temptation to respond quickly may worsen matters.

Garnet in north/Fourth House
Don't let anything stagnate in your home—deal with matters quickly.

Garnet in west/Fifth House
Be philosophical about short-lived relationships or ideas that might come to nothing.

Garnet in Sixth House
You need to tackle matters with more enthusiasm and energy. You could be prone to mild illness.

Garnet in southwest/Seventh House
People in partnerships are likely to irritate you. Try to ignore this, although it may annoy you.

Garnet in Eighth House
Your own anger or that of others could temporarily distract your attention.

Garnet in northeast/Ninth House
Start to explore new possibilities and new horizons.

Garnet in south/Tenth House
You need to be daring, and to move the situation along quickly in order to achieve what you want.

Garnet in northwest/Eleventh House
Take a chance with a new friend or with new group activities, but do not do so in a serious way.

Garnet in Twelfth House
Look closely at your own habits if you find yourself the target of minor accidents or angry outbursts.

Base (root) chakra
Base of spine (perineum)

▲ *Crystals are placed on the base chakra.*

Personality

Garnet represents someone who is busy, obsessive, and somewhat impatient. A live wire, this person will always cause a stir wherever he or she goes—sometimes positive, sometimes negative, but never subtle.

Energy

Active, energetic, unfocused.

Red Jasper

Within the great variety of colors and patterns in jasper is the steady, practical energy of the Earth.

Red Jasper

Color: red mixed with other colors

Hardness: 7

Composition: SiO$_2$ (quartz family)

Qualities: energizing, practical skills

Main chakra: base

▼ *Many different types of stones, including jasper, were traditionally thought to possess the power to ward off attacks from venomous creatures.*

Red jasper forms in veins and slabs from quartz solutions containing hematite, giving it its characteristic brick-red color. This stone is an opaque, microcrystalline variety of quartz. Often, the patterning and color variations in each piece have been created by periods of recrystallization, whereby the rock is fractured and rearranged, usually with other quartz inclusions. Because the structure contains tiny pores, jasper and other quartzes readily take on the color of the surrounding rock.

MYTH AND HISTORY

The meaning of the name "jasper" is unknown, but it is thought to be traceable back to the word *ashpu*, the Assyrian name for the stone. Jasper is frequently mentioned in the Bible, and is listed as one of the foundations of the Heavenly City described in John's vision in *The Book of Revelation*.

Jasper was used for ornaments and amulets throughout the ancient world and Middle Ages. The attraction of the stone was that every piece was unique in its color and markings, yet it could be found in large enough volumes for carving vases, tables, and wall slabs for palaces and churches.

Jasper was also popular in the past as a protection against the bites of snakes and other venomous animals, and against the effects of poison.

SPIRITUAL AND HEALING PROPERTIES

Jasper is earthy, solid, and dependable, and focuses energy at the base chakra in a way that is gently grounding. It encourages practicality and down-to-earth realism. With its many colors and patterns, jasper can also help to stimulate psychic faculties, dreams, and visionary skills, though its main focus is always to repair and enhance the physical structures of the body.

DIVINATORY INTERPRETATION

Wherever jasper appears in a reading, it indicates the need to focus on practical, visible outcomes. Do what is necessary—do not waste time and effort on complicated schemes and elaborate strategies.

Jasper is an opaque stone, and so everything reflected on its surface appears as it really is. This opacity is a signal to take things at face value—nothing is being hidden from you. Devious actions by others will come to nothing if you act honestly and openly. Jasper will also provide sufficient practical skills to accomplish goals, particularly of a physical or material nature.

▶ *This woodcut by Albrecht Dürer depicts a scene from* The Book of Revelation, *which contains many references to gemstones and set a precedent for their use in religious artifacts.*

SUGGESTED READINGS

Red jasper in center/First House
Keep your feet on the ground regardless of what is going on around you.

Red jasper in southeast/Second House
You need to value your skills more and put them to better use.

Red jasper in east/Third House
Be honest in your communications. Bending the truth will only lead to trouble.

Red jasper in north/Fourth House
Take time to finish off day-to-day jobs at home.

Red jasper in west/Fifth House
Leisure time can be used to develop the extra skills that may be needed for future endeavors.

Red jasper in Sixth House
You need to start doing the job at hand—don't question why, just get going.

Red jasper in southwest/Seventh House
Relationships might take more effort than expected. Don't put your partners on pedestals.

Red jasper in Eighth House
Your money should be working for you. Make sure that you are not losing out through careless management.

Red jasper in northeast/Ninth House
Study whichever subjects you want—so long as you can put your knowledge to practical use.

Red jasper in south/Tenth House
Look at the practicalities of your plans for the future and assess whether they are realistic.

Red jasper in northwest/Eleventh House
Be honest with friends and acquaintances and you will reap the benefits.

Red jasper in Twelfth House
Try not to reach for goals that are unattainable. Stick to what you know you can do.

Base (root) chakra
Base of spine (perineum)

▲ *Crystals are placed on the base chakra.*

Personality

The person corresponding to jasper is down-to-earth and straightforward, though by no means simple to define. He or she is good at making useful things, and is not interested in vague dreams or flights of imagination.

Energy

Skillful, practical, down-to-earth.

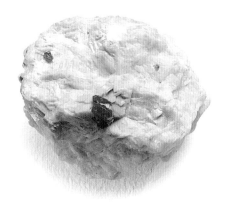

Ruby

Ruby is traditionally thought of as a stone of the heart and of the sun—both the center of our being and the center of our solar system.

Ruby

Color: red

Hardness: 9

Composition: Al_2O_3 + Cr (corundum)

Qualities: balanced, positive, secure

Main chakra: heart

▲ *Gem-quality ruby has the color and translucency of drops of blood, making its link to the life force all the more apparent.*

Ruby is a variety of the hard mineral corundum. The red coloration is caused by small amounts of chromium. It is a difficult stone to imitate well because the color changes depending on the angle of view.

Corundum forms characteristic hexagonal, barrel-shaped crystals, and has been collected from river-bank deposits in southeast Asia for thousands of years. Star ruby is a valuable variation in which tiny crystals of rutile inclusions create an asterism—a starlike refraction of light upon the polished surface of the stone. Synthetic rubies are often used in precision tools such as watches and lasers.

MYTH AND HISTORY

In India, the ruby is the most prized of all gemstones, as it is thought to carry the beneficent energy of the sun. Traditionally, large and transparent rubies were uncommon, and thus symbolized wealth and power. Rubies were associated with the

▲ *Many peoples around the world, particularly from nomadic tribes, wear their wealth in the form of jewelry made from precious metals and adorned with gemstones.*
▲▶ *In the Ayurvedic traditions of India, ruby is the gemstone that holds and amplifies the properties of the sun.*

energy of inextinguishable flame and of inner radiance, and were thought to confer peace, abundance, wealth, and protection. Actually sewn into the flesh, a ruby was thought to make a soldier invulnerable.

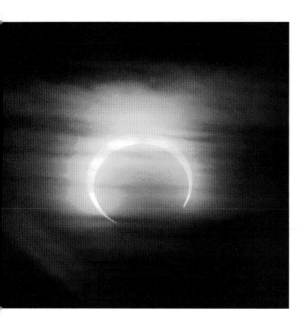

SPIRITUAL AND HEALING PROPERTIES

The physical heart and the heart chakra are the centers of the physical and subtle bodies, and have an important effect on every organ and bodily system. The ruby, which acts on all levels of the heart, is thus an important healing stone. If the heart is truly in balance, everything else follows naturally. A sense of harmony, ease, self-confidence, and clarity of mind are engendered, and these qualities naturally enhance our relationships with others. Star ruby emphasizes the spiritual levels of the heart, the relationship of the individual to the divine, and an increase in the flow of life energy.

DIVINATORY INTERPRETATION

Ruby will have a positive influence wherever it appears in a reading, and will positively affect the stones that are close by. Ruby is supporting, optimistic, and encouraging. It brings a sense of security to all activity, and will imbue everything with a beneficial life-giving energy. In relationships, ruby shows honesty, openness, and

SUGGESTED READINGS

Ruby in center/First House
Make sure to let people know that you are confident and optimistic.

Ruby in southeast/Second House
Be careful with personal finances, but trust that everything will work out.

Ruby in east/Third House
Helpful people surround you, so place your trust in what they offer.

Ruby in north/Fourth House
An infusion of energy and emotion into your home life will help things remain steady.

Ruby in west/Fifth House
You need to be encouraged to take a chance with your own abilities.

Ruby in Sixth House
Confidence at work will carry the situation through for you.

Ruby in southwest/Seventh House
Honesty and openness are needed in all of your relationships.

Ruby in Eighth House
You may be called upon to support someone emotionally or financially, or you may need help yourself.

Ruby in northeast/Ninth House
Keep looking at the positive side of events.

Ruby in south/Tenth House
Sudden changes of plans and direction are unwise. Stick to tried and successful ideas.

Ruby in northwest/Eleventh House
Friends may ask for your support now to help give them the confidence they need.

Ruby in Twelfth House
Quiet periods spent alone are needed to sustain you through this busy time and to help keep your stress levels low.

Heart chakra
Center of breastbone in center of chest

▲ *Crystals are placed on the heart chakra.*

levels of emotional harmony; in work and everyday life, ruby shows contentment and self-confidence. In health matters, ruby may suggest the need to look after the heart, physically or emotionally, especially if situated near other warning stones.

Personality

A ruby personality is open, warm, friendly, and confident. This person is a natural leader who shows responsibility for others, and is honest and trustworthy.

Energy

Encouraging, helpful, sustaining.

Tiger's Eye

Tiger's eye is a striking stone with a lively play of different colors. It is a form of quartz in which the original fibers of asbestos or crocodilite have been replaced by parallel quartz bands.

Tiger's eye

Color: yellow to brown, with occasional bands of red and blue

Hardness: 7

Composition: SiO_2 (silicon dioxide)

Qualities: grounding, confidence-building

Main chakras: base, sacral, solar plexus

▲▶ *Cat's eye stones can occur in several different types of mineral, where inclusions create a line of light. The qualities of large cats such as the tiger and the leopard suggest that such stones confer stealth, strength, nobility, and grace to the wearer.*

Tiger's eye has graded bands of yellow and golden brown in various shades. Passing through these bands are parallel silky fibers that have a wonderful sheen as they catch and reflect the light. The orange and yellow tones are created by iron inclusions which, if they come into contact with heat, will turn to the deep red color of hematite.

MYTH AND HISTORY

Tiger's eye is an attractive stone that is usually cut as a "cabochon," a smooth, rounded dome that enhances its natural luster. Original sources were India and Burma; South Africa and Australia are now important sources as well.

A blue variety of tiger's eye known as hawk's eye or falcon's eye—in which less iron is present in the quartz fibers—also exists. In the valuable cat's-eye stones, light reflects from minute fibers within the transparent crystal in a bright line. Tiger's eye is similar in appearance to these stones but, being opaque, is less valuable.

SPIRITUAL AND HEALING PROPERTIES

Because of its range of colors, tiger's eye is an excellent stone to balance all three lower chakras: base, sacral, and solar plexus. With its fibrous striations, it is able to balance the flow of energy between these centers, thus encouraging confidence, practicality, and an ability to feel at home in the world. Tiger's eye is gently grounding, but the scintillating play of light suggests lightness of touch and an appreciation of joy and beauty, as well as the ability to receive intuitive flashes of information.

DIVINATORY INTERPRETATION

Tiger's eye has a positive, helpful energy bringing confidence and a practical ability to achieve success. It indicates the need to take a practical, down-to-earth approach to problems or issues. Start with fundamentals and with what you know, and work slowly and methodically from there. Tiger's eye definitely suggests that you shouldn't try to go it alone. We all need help and advice from others, and this stone implies that now is the time to work in groups toward a common objective.

▼ *The qualities of tiger's eye are epitomized by those who spend their lives working within tightly organized social groups, where sociability and practicality are essential.*

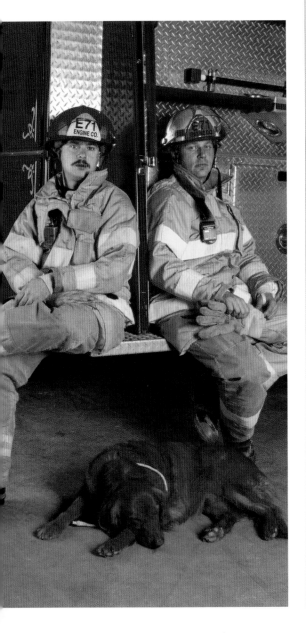

SUGGESTED READINGS

Tiger's eye in center/First House
Be open to working with others, especially those offering practical help.

Tiger's eye in southeast/Second House
Don't rely on your own resources alone to help you in this situation.

Tiger's eye in east/Third House
Talk to others about your ideas. Consider their opinions before you do anything.

Tiger's eye in north/Fourth House
It's time to ask older, more experienced family members for advice and guidance.

Tiger's eye in west/Fifth House
You need to take some risks if you want to succeed.

Tiger's eye in Sixth House
What is needed now is a methodical and steady approach to work, with no sudden changes.

Tiger's eye in southwest/Seventh House
Partnerships and relationships may need extra loving care and attention at the moment.

Tiger's eye in Eighth House
Be cautious where corporate finance is concerned, or where other people have control over your money.

Tiger's eye in northeast/Ninth House
At present there is a possibility for study or travel with friends. Long journeys connected with celebrations may lie ahead.

Tiger's eye in south/Tenth House
Look at the plans you have made for the future and check that you haven't left anything out.

Tiger's eye in northwest/Eleventh House
See if you can involve yourself in a group that shares your goals.

Tiger's eye in Twelfth House
It would be helpful to take part in group activities in which you can forget all the pressures you are under for a while.

Solar plexus chakra
Midway between navel and base of ribs

Sacral chakra
Midway between navel and pubic bone

Base (root) chakra
Base of spine (perineum)

▲ *Crystals are placed on the solar plexus, sacral, and base chakras.*

Personality

Tiger's eye suggests a warm, sociable, practical person with a good sense of humor. This person may need to always be around people in order to feel comfortable.

Energy

Sociable, practical, group-oriented.

Hematite

Hematite is seen as the sacred blood of the Earth Mother herself, and has been valued for longer than any other mineral.

Hematite

Color: metallic silver-gray to brick red

Hardness: 5–6

Composition: Fe_2O_3 (iron oxide)

Qualities: grounding, solidity

Main chakra: base

Hematite is a common mineral forming in igneous rock from iron-rich water. Crystals are uncommon; more often, hematite forms kidney-shaped masses. The high iron content of this mineral makes it an important industrial source of iron.

MYTH AND HISTORY

Hundreds of thousands of years before the smelting of iron was discovered, hematite ore was a major trade item. In its metallic form, it was used for jewelry and ornaments, but most precious was the fine-grained ocher—an earthy iron-rich compound used as a sacred red pigment. The oldest mines known are in South Africa, where the hematite was laboriously dug out of open pits with wood and bone picks. These mines were in

◄ *The use of red pigment is one of the most ancient methods of denoting the ritually prepared or sanctified individual.*

▲ *Fairy tales and folk legends instruct us on the attractions and pitfalls of entering the spirit world unprepared. In this realm, iron is one of the main protections against harm.*

continuous use for many thousands of years. Once a pit was exhausted, it was carefully refilled to restore the sacred place to its original state.

The graves and bones of Neanderthal man have been found packed in red ocher, suggesting that, even at this early time, man recognized the spiritual symbolism of this life-giving blood of Mother Earth. Hematite continues to be an important source of red pigment today.

SPIRITUAL AND HEALING PROPERTIES

With its iron content, hematite has a strengthening influence on the physical body—especially the blood, body temperature, and circulatory system. Of all the grounding stones, hematite is perhaps the surest—very few people fail to be brought down to a steady, focused state due to its stabilizing influence on the physical body.

Traditionally, iron was held to be the only protection against the Faerie Kingdoms, and today, hematite will prevent you from being taken "away with the fairies" or, to use another colloquialism for an unfocused mind, being "spaced out."

When used by a fully balanced personality, hematite can provide access to spirit travel and astral worlds.

DIVINATORY INTERPRETATION

Iron is a strong but brittle metal, and these characteristics provide a clue to its divinatory meanings. Hematite appearing in a cast will show solid foundations upon which to build. In a positive placement, it will encourage the solidification of other energies close to it. In this way, hematite can crystallize a situation so that it becomes clear and visible to all. In a negative placement, hematite can indicate stubbornness, inflexibility, or an inability to move away from a current condition.

Hematite appears to be a shiny silver metal, but when powdered, it becomes red. This transformation shows us that it is sometimes necessary to look beyond the surface of matters.

Hematite in center/First House
You have a need to be seen by others as strong, dependable, and loyal.

Hematite in southeast/Second House
Unwillingness to change a point of view could be clouding issues at the moment.

Hematite in east/Third House
Straight talking is needed to maintain your position, even if you are unsure of the views of others.

Hematite in north/Fourth House
Take time to repair those items in your home that keep it secure.

Hematite in west/Fifth House
You need to put more effort into your leisure time if you wish to actually do the things you keep thinking about.

Hematite in Sixth House
Commit yourself to tackling work with more flexibility.

Hematite in southwest/Seventh House
Secure relationships can become boring. Make sure you are not taking others for granted.

Hematite in Eighth House
Any change in your financial situation should be carefully examined.

Hematite in northeast/Ninth House
Time to consolidate, not expand into new areas. Slow things down!

Hematite in south/Tenth House
Your ability to integrate your skills has helped you to get what you want.

Hematite in northwest/Eleventh House
Don't try to deceive your friends—they know you too well. Just be you.

Hematite in Twelfth House
Look beyond the obvious to find the strength and security you need.

Base (root) chakra
*Base of spine
(perineum)*

▲ *Crystals are placed on the base chakra.*

Personality

This crystal can represent someone who is solid and dependable, if a little too down-to-earth at times. This person may appear boring, but he or she has a strengthening and stabilizing effect on those around them. He or she may have access to spiritual experiences, but will keep this a secret.

Hematite energy

Strong, secure, straightforward

Pyrite

Pyrite (or iron pyrites) is commonly known as "fool's gold." For those who know its secrets, it can point the way to finding real gold.

Pyrite

Color: metallic yellow

Hardness: 6.5

Composition: FeS_2
(iron sulfide)

Qualities: cleansing, clearing

Main chakra: solar plexus

▲▶ *Pyrite is one of the few common minerals capable of creating fire. Flint and quartz will spark if struck strongly, but pyrite, being softer, is much easier to use.*
▶ *The association of pyrite with the sun and fire made it an important material in many ancient cultures. It was particularly valued by Central American civilizations, which tended to focus their ritual worship on the sun and the stars.*

Pyrite is formed when water comes into contact with extremely hot rocks. It usually occurs in granular or massive form, but sometimes crystals of striking cubic appearance are formed. Pyrite creates sulfuric acid as it decomposes, which is exploited industrially. It is also used in paints and polishes. Bits of copper and gold can sometimes occur within pyrites.

MYTH AND HISTORY

The name of this stone comes from the Greek word *pyr*, meaning fire. When struck or broken, pyrite gives off sparks, and thus it was used in ancient times as a fire-making tool—the ancient precursor to sulfur-dipped matches. Because it shines like the sun and makes fire, we can guess that pyrite must have been a powerful spiritual artifact. The most important spirit for protection and warmth, the perception

of fire living within a stone would certainly have made a great impression on our ancestors.

In many ancient civilizations, pyrite was used as a healing amulet, as it was thought to prevent "blood decay." In the civilizations of Central and South America, the Aztecs and Incas cut and polished slabs of pyrite into convex mirrors, many of which were placed in tombs.

SPIRITUAL AND HEALING PROPERTIES

Pyrite is a combination of iron and sulfur, two important elements for maintaining the physical health of the body. Iron is an essential ingredient of the blood, without which absorption of oxygen into cells becomes impossible. Sulfur is a constituent of amino acids and proteins—the smell of burning hair is primarily sulfur.

Pyrite also helps to regulate the digestive system. Through gentle cleansing action, it is a detoxifying agent that helps protect from pollution and negative forms of energy. Anxiety, frustration, and depression can all be eased using pyrite.

DIVINATION INTERPRETATION

The shining, mirrorlike surface of pyrite can reveal what is around it, yet can itself be deceptive. What appears to be golden may in fact be something completely different. Thus, when pyrite appears in a cast, be cautious of appearances. Things are definitely not what they seem, although this deception may not be conscious or malicious.

The nature of some things is to reflect what is around them—our reactions to this reflection often reveal more about ourselves than does the mirror itself. When pyrite appears in a reading, we should ask ourselves what is being mirrored back to us that we find uncomfortable. The lesson of pyrite is to act with awareness—not to simply react to what happens to us. Clear out the debris that clutters your life and prevents you from reflecting your true brightness. In a positive position, pyrite can show itself as an initiator, bringing a spark of inspiration or a sudden clarity of insight. But again, such a spark needs to be carefully examined for its true meaning and value.

▶ *Pyrite is so common in the Earth's crust that it is found in almost every possible environment, hence its vast number of forms and varieties.*

SUGGESTED READINGS

Pyrite in center/First House
You may not appear to others as you hope to.

Pyrite in southeast/Second House
It is time to indulge yourself in order to relieve current pressures.

Pyrite in east/Third House
Others could easily misunderstand your intentions, so be cautious to whom you speak.

Solar plexus chakra
Midway between navel and base of ribs

Pyrite in north/Fourth House
Consider spring cleaning or space clearing at home or in any other personal space.

▲ *Crystals are placed on the solar plexus chakra.*

Pyrite in west/Fifth House
Set aside quiet time to escape into imagined worlds created by yourself or others.

Pyrite in Sixth House
Clutter and garbage of all kinds—both physical and mental—must be thrown out if you wish to clarify present issues.

Pyrite in southwest/Seventh House
Concerns within relationships and partnerships need to be smoothed over.

Pyrite in Eighth House
Be cautious in any financial dealings; check the details and any advice given.

Pyrite in northeast/Ninth House
Rely on your own experience rather than on those who would impress you with their expertise and knowledge.

Pyrite in south/Tenth House
Reexamine the various jobs you are doing at the moment and cut out those that do not support you.

Pyrite in northwest/Eleventh House
Friends need your compassion and understanding.

Pyrite in Twelfth House
Take time out to reflect on everything that is happening right now.

Personality

The pyrite personality is usually difficult to get to know. He or she may be a braggart or simply a dreamer. Shattering the illusion might produce a quick, fiery response.

Energy

Soothing, cleansing, deceptive.

A m b e r

Amber is thought to carry the energy of warm sunlight within its translucent depths.

Amber

Color: yellow, yellow-red, red, green

Hardness: 2–2.5

Composition: complex hydrocarbons (fossil resin)

Qualities: warming, stimulating

Main chakra: solar plexus

Amber reflects the very beginnings of the planet Earth, for it is the fossilized resin that dripped from the pine trees of the forests that grew in the Tertiary Period, over 50 million years ago. Damaged trees leaked resins that fell to the forest floor and were then covered by deep sediments of sands and gravel. After millions of years, erosion washed the amber nodules down to the sea, where they eventually washed up on coastlines.

MYTH AND HISTORY

Amber is found in various parts of the world, including Germany, Canada, and the USA, but the Baltic Sea coasts are its most famous source.

Because it is light and easily worked, amber has been a valuable jewel for thousands of years. Although most amber is cloudy, this cloudiness often clears with gentle heat. Classical poets described amber as the tears of gods, or as the essence of the rays of the setting sun washed up on the sea shore. Amber was

also prized in the Roman Empire. The Emperor Nero even mounted an expedition to the Baltic coast to gather his own supplies. In many ancient civilizations, amulets and medicines were commonly made with amber, as it dissolves readily in alcohol.

▲ *Amber has long been a favored material for making beads. Worked amber beads have been found in Stone Age burial sites in Scandanavia and Britain.*

SPIRITUAL AND HEALING PROPERTIES

Amber is known as having electrical properties—static electricity is generated when a piece is rubbed. It is thus no surprise that it benefits the electrical systems of the body. Amber can improve the functions of the brain and nervous system, release anxiety, and increase clarity of mind. It is a stimulating compound, but some may find that

▲ *Some classical philosophers believed amber to be fossilized tree resin. Others, less accurately, believed it to be the solidified urine of lynxes.*

wearing it for longer than an hour creates irritation or overactivity. It can also be useful for detoxification, and can alleviate depression.

DIVINATORY INTERPRETATION

Amber inserts a certain degree of nervous energy into its surroundings. If found in a placement where other indicators show restriction, stagnancy, and doubt, it acts as a stimulus to get things moving. In a positive or already balanced placement, its presence signals that the questioner needs to take care that things don't get overexcited and frenetic. Amber is like a gemstone caffeine—too much will create chaos, bad temper, and arguments. As long as this excess energy can be used, however, problems will not usually arise.

Where amber appears, watch for skills being underused, for emotions being repressed, and for unalleviated anxieties and tensions.

SUGGESTED READINGS

Amber in center/First House
An atmosphere of enthusiasm and boundless energy is needed to bring order to the situation.

Amber in southeast/Second House
You have a renewed drive to cope with personal finances and to pull your life together.

Amber in east/Third House
There may be too much talking and not enough listening to other people.

Amber in north/Fourth House
Right now is a busy time at home. A lot of things are happening at once.

Amber in west/Fifth House
You have a myriad of ideas for projects—keep a note of each one so you can review them in quieter times.

Amber in Sixth House
Nervousness and restlessness for long periods of time can cause health problems. Learn to relax.

Amber in southwest/Seventh House
Over-intellectualizing can lead to disagreements when emotions are not considered.

Amber in Eighth House
The current rapid pace of events may cause you stress, or may leave you feeling full of energy.

Solar plexus Chakra
Midway between navel and base of ribs

Amber in northeast/Ninth House
Don't take the first opportunity that presents itself. Think things through before committing to anything.

Amber in south/Tenth House
Your energy needs to be focused more carefully—you may have too many projects going on at once.

Amber in northwest/Eleventh House
You have many events to attend and people to meet.

Amber in Twelfth House
Sleep may be temporarily shallow and fitful.

▲ *Crystals are placed on the solar plexus chakra.*

◄ *In essence, amber is the live energy of trees captured in a stable form, then fossilized for millions of years. This unique means of formation gives amber the ability to generate an extraordinary amount of energy.*

Personality

Amber personalities are always on the go. They are intelligent and aware, but often find it difficult to sit still or relax. They have a tendency to work too hard and they worry a lot.

Energy

Enlivening, stimulating, electric.

Citrine

Citrine is a transparent yellow variety of quartz crystal that is valued as much for its warm color as for its rarity.

Citrine occurs naturally where quartz recrystallizes with iron inclusions. It can vary in tone from a deep brown-orange to a pale lemon color.

Citrine

Color: yellow, golden brown, orange-brown

Hardness: 7

Composition: SiO_2 (quartz)

Qualities: uplifting, warming, confident

Main chakra: solar plexus

▲ *Natural yellow citrine is rare, and so most commercial stones, such as those used for jewelry making, are actually heat-treated amethysts.*

MYTH AND HISTORY

Because of its rarity and delicacy of color, citrine has long been a valuable gemstone. The pale varieties can resemble other precious stones such as heliodor (yellow beryl), chrysoberyl, and some varieties of topaz. During the Middle Ages, citrine was thought to carry the energy of the sun's rays, and thus it was used as a remedy for people whose energy and moods became depressed during the long winter months or during overcast weather.

SPIRITUAL AND HEALING PROPERTIES

Citrine's wide range of colors enables it to help balance many different areas of the physical and subtle bodies. The deep orange-brown varieties help to energize the base chakra, and have a gentle grounding effect. Orange-yellow stones work well at the sacral chakra, helping the body to release stress and tension and enjoy life

◄ *When the solar plexus chakra is balanced by citrine, one will find plenty of energy, optimism, and an exuberant enjoyment of life.*

more. Most effective is yellow citrine, which acts at the solar plexus, balancing the digestive and nervous systems and bringing clarity and focus to the mind. It is gently expansive, relaxing, and comforting, increasing self-confidence and personal power. The golden tones within the crystal also relate to the spiritual energies above the crown of the head, bringing higher levels of wisdom and knowledge. As a grounding stone, citrine helps integrate these levels of intuition into everyday life.

DIVINATORY INTERPRETATION

Citrine brings confidence, the energy to succeed, and a clarity of mind and purpose. It will always help to bring together different energies, particularly if there is a conflict between desire and reality, between an idealist and a pragmatist, or between relaxation and action.

In situations that lack clarity, citrine will bring in the light of the sun to illuminate the problems in such a way as to allow them to be seen for what they are. Citrine requires that thoughts precede actions; thinking the situation through will bring both understanding and the information needed to succeed. Ignoring this stage of the process will likely cause anxiety and confusion.

In a difficult placement, citrine may counsel caution. It can also advise to take things step by step, ensuring that the foundation beneath each step is solid before continuing.

▶ *Faceted citrine quartz displays a full range of brilliant, warm tones.*

SUGGESTED READINGS

Citrine in center/First House
An image of confidence will help all situations at this time.

Citrine in southeast/Second House
Take comfort in steady, predictable routines that are supportive of present needs.

Citrine in east/Third House
Be clear about all types of communication, even if you have to repeat yourself.

Citrine in north/Fourth House
The roots of the issue are sound and settled, and will provide plenty of security.

Citrine in west/Fifth House
You need to set aside time to relax and have some fun.

Citrine in Sixth House
Look on the bright side of current events to give you the lift you need.

Citrine in southwest/Seventh House
Comfort and kind words from partners will help dissolve anxieties.

Citrine in Eighth House
People with deep concerns find you approachable and easy to talk to, but don't become too involved in their problems.

Citrine in northeast/Ninth House
Your thoughts on the larger situation are correct, so trust your perceptions and intuition.

Citrine in south/Tenth House
The issue can be confidently pushed farther along its path, as long as you consider the well-being of others.

Citrine in northwest/Eleventh House
Quiet times with friends will boost your confidence and calm unnecessary worries.

Citrine in Twelfth House
Dreams and insights will confirm your present direction.

Solar plexus chakra
Midway between
navel and base of ribs

▲ *Crystals are placed on the solar plexus chakra.*

Personality

The citrine personality is happy, confident, and sunny. These people have a practical side, but they also like to explore the subtle realms of mind and spirit.

Energy

Comforting, uplifting, happy.

Blue Lace Agate

The delicate and subtle bandings within this crystal make it one of the rarest and most popular of the agates.

Blue lace agate

Color: bands of blue and white

Hardness: 6.5

Composition: SiO_2 (agate quartz)

Qualities: calming, uplifting

Main chakra: throat

▲▶ *Agate was a popular stone for carving until modern times. This late eighteenth-century vase was created from a single piece of highly decorative agate.*

Technically, agates are a type of chalcedony quartz, but they are often separately identified because of the distinct bands of microcrystalline layers. Blue lace agate is considered a variety of quartz, albeit an uncommon one.

Agates commonly form when volcanic rocks containing crevices and cavities become filled with quartz solutions as they cool. Each layer of agate crystallizes differently, depending on conditions, temperature, and impurities present, so that agate sizes and colors vary, and a distinctive banding is created. When not completely filled with bands of microcrystals, the center of an agate can contain clear quartz, amethyst, or smoky quartz crystals.

As agate is harder than the surrounding bedrock, it can often be found in topsoil and on beaches as individual nodules.

MYTH AND HISTORY

Agate was highly valued by many ancient civilizations, including the Egyptians and Sumerians, even though today it is regarded only as a semi-precious stone. It was named by the Greek scholar Theophrastus in the third century BC after the river Achates, located in present-day Sicily, where it was first discovered. The Greeks became renowned for their skills in carving agate, and some of their most famous artists used the stone, including Pyrgoteles, the engraver of Alexander the Great.

In the Roman Empire, agate was used for all sorts of decorative carving and jewelry, including seal rings, which originally only the upper classes were allowed to own. When it could be cut to show concentric circles, it was valued as a remedy for the evil eye. Even without this particular patterning, agate was thought to strengthen all virtues and provide protection from harm.

▲ *This agate cameo displays the profile of Alexander the Great with the rams' horns of the Egyptian god Amun.*

SPIRITUAL AND HEALING PROPERTIES

The blue of this variety of agate is both striking and delicate. The color strengthens the function of the throat chakra and, like all blue stones, encourages peace, calm, and a sense of quiet detachment. Blue lace agate can be of use wherever there is aggravation or a build-up of energy causing pain, irritation, or inflammation. The energy of blue lace agate is much softer than that of many other blue stones—it tends to be uplifting and supporting, and its subtle variations can suggest the influence of higher spiritual realms.

DIVINATORY INTERPRETATION

Blue lace agate in a reading suggests that many levels of communication are needed, or are going on within the area of the cast. This communication is neither frenetic nor frantic in nature, nor is it necessarily characterized by conflict or argument. The stone's presence simply indicates that there are different ways of understanding and sharing experiences, and that in order to make the most of the situation it is best to acknowledge this fact. This stone also suggests a need be open to communications from unexpected places.

In general, blue lace agate will show an easygoing, light, and enjoyable situation in which communication is important.

SUGGESTED READINGS

Blue lace agate in center/First House
Be more aware of what your body language and mannerisms may be indicating to others.

Blue lace agate in southeast/Second House
Your beliefs about a situation may be impeding your judgment.

Blue lace agate in east/Third House
Be willing to listen to others and to hear what they are saying.

Blue lace agate in north/Fourth House
You really are secure and safe.

Blue lace agate in west/Fifth House
Spend more time in easy conversation and try to enjoy yourself more often.

Blue lace agate in Sixth House
If you feel your health is not as it should be, then do something positive about it.

Blue lace agate in southwest/Seventh House
Be willing to share your thoughts with those who are close to you.

Blue lace agate in Eighth House
Make more of an effort to understand other people's problems.

Blue lace agate in northeast/Ninth House
Make sure you have properly understood the message before you try to pass it on to others.

Blue lace agate in south/Tenth House
Express yourself clearly, to avoid confusion.

Blue lace agate in northwest/Eleventh House
You do not need to believe what everyone else may be saying. Go your own way.

Blue lace agate in Twelfth House
Listen to what your dreams seem to be telling you at the moment.

Throat chakra
Neck

▲ *Crystals are placed on the throat chakra.*

Personality

This person is perhaps a little vague. He or she is spiritually oriented, and is likely a dreamer as well as a good communicator.

Energy

Communicator, listener.

Azurite

Electric-blue azurite crystals have long been a valuable source of pigment for artists.

Azurite

Color: blue, dark blue

Hardness: 3.5–4

Composition:
$Cu_3(CO_3)_2(OH)_2$

Qualities: integration, consciousness, understanding

Main chakra: brow

▲ *Traditionally, the intense blue color of azurtite insured its use as a pigment for making paints.*

Azurite is a secondary mineral, forming from the oxidation of copper ores. Over time, as it absorbs water, it changes into the green mineral malachite. The two minerals are thus often found together in the ground, and can form an azurite-malachite rock that is blue-green in color.

Crystals of azurite are rare but extremely beautiful, with deep blue blades catching the light on their edges, and showing a stunning, electric-blue color. Most commonly, azurite appears as a powdery concretion in a lighter, forget-me-not shade of blue. Although an ore of copper, azurite is rarely used as a commercial source of that metal.

MYTH AND HISTORY

Azurite is named for its color, "azure" blue. Ancient metalworkers and miners would have recognized this mineral, and would likely have known that workable copper could probably be found nearby.

Azurite has been used as an ornamental stone and a gemstone despite its softness, simply because of its wonderful color. When found together with malachite, azurite tends to be a little more robust.

In the early Middle Ages and early Renaissance, azurite was used to make blue pigments called "mountain blue" and "Armenian stone." Over time, these pigments can collect water and change from blue to green, which is why many of the paintings from the thirteenth century have such an unusual color scheme today.

SPIRITUAL AND HEALING PROPERTIES

The dark brilliance of azurite speeds the vibration of all energies toward the spiritual realm. Blue stones tend to be quietening and cooling, but azurite has a shifting, transformative quality. It is also known to stimulate deep levels of consciousness, and to increase subtle communication skills such as intuition, creativity, and inspiration. Understanding is also encouraged.

Azurite also has the ability to release deep stresses, and can help heal ailments caused by a breakdown of communication between different bodily systems. Security and an increased ease of energy flow make azurite an important stone for healers, as well as for those who wish to develop their own healing skills.

DIVINATORY INTERPRETATION

Azurite in a reading will bring swift results to the area in which it appears. It has the ability to smooth over and transform difficult and rigid circumstances, encouraging understanding and acceptance at deep healing levels.

In areas of conflict, azurite suggests that a resolution is within reach. It will bring a deepening level of awareness, establishing a quiet but dynamic stability and assuredness. In situations that have been locked or stuck, azurite suggests that changes are about to occur, and that a newer, more creative flow of energy is about to begin.

Azurite tells us as well that increased communication and understanding can bring forth a deep empathy which may help to resolve conflict. Transformation and change may also occur, so it is necessary to remain both flexible and aware.

SUGGESTED READINGS

Azurite in center/First House
Try to be more open to the opinion of others.

Azurite in southeast/Second House
Allow change to happen, even though you are uncertain of the outcome.

Azurite in east/Third House
Keep things running smoothly with prompt communications.

Azurite in north/Fourth House
Try to relax, even though events may be moving faster than you feel comfortable with.

Azurite in west/Fifth House
Take time to explore activities that bring a sense of peace.

Azurite in Sixth House
The giving or receiving of a healing touch is required at the moment.

Azurite in southwest/Seventh House
This is a time to be close to those you care about. Listen to their concerns.

Azurite in Eighth House
Sensitivity to others' feelings will help you pinpoint areas that need healing.

Azurite in northeast/Ninth House
Make it your goal to learn more about healing techniques that interest you.

Azurite in south/Tenth House
You need to seriously consider a complete change of direction and a transformation of your goals.

Azurite in northwest/Eleventh House
Lingering unresolved issues need to be dealt with.

Azurite in Twelfth House
Experiment with techniques that calm the mind and relax the body.

Brow chakra
Center of forehead

▲ *Crystals are placed on the brow chakra.*

Personality

The azurite person is a healer—perhaps by profession, or perhaps in everyday behavior with others. This person can always lift a situation to the highest possible level, and is both mysterious and enigmatic.

Energy

Healing, transformative, empathetic.

◀ *The Virgin Mary, dressed in blue robes, is an archetypal image of a healer. With its rich blue coloration, azurite is an important stone for healers.*

L a p i s
L a z u l i

Lapis lazuli is a precious deep-blue rock containing lazurite, along with other minerals.

Lapis lazuli

Color: deep blue with white and gold flecks

Hardness: 5.5

Composition: $(Na, Ca)_8$ $(Al. Si)_{12} O_{24} (S,SO_4)$ (sodium aluminosilicate with sulfur)

Qualities: consciousness, memory, meditation

Main chakras: throat, brow

▲▶ *The ceremonial vestments of the Egyptian pharoahs were often adorned with lapis lazuli, which was seen as a symbol of divine justice.*
▶▶ *Cosmic balance and personal virtue were united in Egyptian beliefs regarding the soul's journey in the afterlife. Lapis lazuli was thought to help the dead pass safely through their trials.*

Lapis lazuli forms when limestone comes into contact with calcite and pyrite, creating a new, deep-blue mineral known as lazurite. A rock rather than a single mineral, lapis usually consists of compact lazurite crystals peppered with white dolomite, calcite, grains of pyrite, and sodalite. Lazurite crystals by themselves are less common than lapis lazuli rock.

MYTH AND HISTORY

The best source for lapis lazuli has always been Afghanistan, where the finest deep-blue stones are mined. Chile is a good source as well; other sites include Italy, Russia, and Argentina.

The name of this precious stone derives from the Latin for stone, *lapis*, and the Persian name of the mineral, *lajuward*, from which the word "azure" also derives. Some ancient authorities used the name *sapphirus* or "sapphire" when talking about lapis.

Called *chesbet* by the ancient Egyptians, lapis lazuli was sacred to Maat, the goddess of truth and balance, and was worn by the chief priest to invoke that goddess's power of justice. The Egyptians also used lapis lazuli to carve scarabs and cylinders, as well as for decorating royal vestments and temples. Roman soldiers wore lapis lazuli scarabs in rings for courage and protection. The stone was also ground up to make the pigment known as ultramarine.

SPIRITUAL AND HEALING PROPERTIES

Lapis lazuli is a deep balancer, and works especially well with the brow and throat areas. It can remove deep levels of stress and trauma from the system, although some discomfort during the clearing process may be experienced.

Lapis brings the spiritual qualities of deep silence and perspective that can be unnerving to those unfamiliar with these sensations. It is in this space, however, that profound intuition and inspiration can arise.

Lapis lazuli can also help access levels of universal truth and balance that reach far beyond individual concepts of right and wrong, and is excellent for the healing of deep or chronic wounds of all sorts.

DIVINATORY INTERPRETATION

In a reading, lapis lazuli shows that truth is essential in the situation if success is to be achieved. Honesty, straightforward communication, and clarity will allow all energies to flow easily. It may also reveal the necessity to dig deep in order to uncover the truth of a situation. As a stone of the goddess of truth and balance, in some instances it may show the workings of law and order in society.

A stone of teaching, lapis lazuli may also indicate a time of study or of learning. In a position related to individual spirituality, it shows deep reflection, meditation, working with the distant past, and significant memories. Wherever it appears, lapis lazuli is a sobering, balancing, and profound influence.

SUGGESTED READINGS

Lapis lazuli in center/First House
It is important that you be impartial and fair in your dealings.

Lapis lazuli in southeast/Second House
Be cautious when judging people or situations by your own standards.

Lapis lazuli in east/Third House
Do not get drawn into gossiping about others.

Lapis lazuli in north/Fourth House
Distant memories may be very helpful in putting current events into perspective.

Lapis lazuli in west/Fifth House
Take time out to appreciate the beauty of natural surroundings.

Lapis lazuli in Sixth House
Don't rush into sudden decisions without first making sure you have all the facts.

Lapis lazuli in southwest/Seventh House
Honesty is needed from both partners in a current relationship.

Lapis lazuli in Eighth House
It will take some effort to uncover the truth of the situation.

Lapis lazuli in northeast/Ninth House
You need to stand up for the truth, even if this means you will be standing alone.

Lapis lazuli in south/Tenth House
Don't step on people to achieve your goals. The consequences will damage your ambitions.

Lapis lazuli in northwest/Eleventh House
Be careful to avoid excess of all kinds in your social life.

Lapis lazuli in Twelfth House
You need to find a peaceful space away from the busy world.

Brow chakra
Center of forehead

Throat chakra
Neck

▲ *Crystals are placed on the brow and throat chakras.*

Personality

The lapis lazuli person is a serious, deep thinker, perhaps a teacher of some kind, but at an advanced level. He or she may also be involved with the law.

Energy

Truthful, serious.

Sodalite

Sodalite can be easily confused with its relative, lapis lazuli. The two crystals are sometimes found together.

Sodalite

Color: deep blue with white veins and inclusions

Hardness: 5.5–6

Composition: $Na_4Al_3Si_3O_{12}Cl$ (aluminosilicate of sodium with chlorine)

Qualities: peaceful, clarifying, perceptive

Main chakras: throat, brow

▲▶ *An important stone for all types of communication, sodalite encourages understanding, clarity, and truth, and can help support those who engage in long-distant communications on a consistent basis.*

Sodalite derives its name from its high sodium content, and is related to several other aluminosilicates with very similar structures. It is commonly found in massive, microcrystalline form; crystals are rare. The deep-blue varieties have long been popular as gemstones, and are sometimes used as an alternative to lapis lazuli, although sodalite can be distinguished from lapis lazuli fairly easily by its white veining, its slightly darker blue color, and its lack of pyrites.

MYTH AND HISTORY

Sodalite was not identified as a separate mineral until the nineteenth century. It has, however, been used for many centuries for making beads. No doubt it would have been named "sapphire" in the Middle Ages, as virtually all deep-blue gemstones were.

SPIRITUAL AND HEALING PROPERTIES

Sodalite works well in unison with the throat and brow chakras. It is a clarifying stone that balances the emotions and steadies the thought processes. Like all deep-blue stones, it will bring a deep level of peace, and thus can be a useful aid to meditation and contemplation.

The white veining in sodalite is suggestive of communications with far-flung parts of the universe. Sodalite also helps to support the lymphatic system, and thus the immune functions of the body. Its high sodium content benefits the body's fluid systems.

DIVINATORY INTERPRETATION

The appearance of sodalite in a reading indicates communication on a large scale—both between different peoples and between distant countries. Messages are being sent and received using many methods, including wires, cables, and satellites—even telepathically, between minds.

Sodalite also acts as a mediator and peace-bringer, and its appearance in a reading represents a meeting of minds. Expect news that will bring resolutions and new opportunities, but you must be ready to play your part. If you are not receiving the messages you expect, it may be necessary to contact others involved in the situation and to keep talking about the issue.

Sodalite in a reading can also suggest a state of peace and contentment, but not one of isolation. You may be by yourself, but you will not feel alone. This can be an ideal opportunity for research and study.

SUGGESTED READINGS

Sodalite in center/First House
You may find yourself in the role of mediator or peace-broker.

Brow chakra
Center of forehead

Throat chakra
Neck

Sodalite in south-east/Second House
Learn to accept yourself as you are.

Sodalite in east/Third House
Be prepared to act as the go-between for various groups of people.

Sodalite in north/Fourth House
Do what you can to create peace at home.

▲ *Crystals are placed on the brow and throat chakras.*

Sodalite in west/Fifth House
You have plenty of time for relaxation and leisure. Enjoy yourself.

Sodalite in Sixth House
New opportunities at work need to be firmly grasped.

Sodalite in southwest/Seventh House
Listen to what others are saying before expressing your own opinions.

Sodalite in Eighth House
Others may be tempting you to take up new financial commitments. Think hard before you do anything and don't overextend yourself.

Sodalite in northeast/Ninth House
Make sure that your message is being heard by as many people as possible.

Sodalite in south/Tenth House
Be prepared to expand your horizons further than you had ever thought possible.

Sodalite in northwest/Eleventh House
You may be expected to resolve disputes by talking to everyone involved.

Sodalite in Twelfth House
Pay attention to your instincts, intuition, and dreams.

Personality
A typical sodalite individual has strong links to communication technologies. His or her primary interest likely lies in the exchange of information. This person is also emotionally restrained and self-possessed.

Energy
Mediator, communicator.

Flint

Flint tools such as arrowheads and axes are among the earliest examples of prehistoric technology.

Flint

Color: blue-gray, gray, black

Hardness: 7

Composition: SiO_2

Qualities: strengthening, regenerating

Main chakra: solar plexus

Flint is a variety of quartz that is created on sea beds when limestone hardens into nodules, or when it is replaced by silica. Because of this origin, it is commonly found together with chalk and the remains of ancient microscopic sea creatures, and may itself contain fossils. Dark gray in color, flint weathers to a white crust upon exposure to air.

MYTH AND HISTORY

The name for this mineral may derive from the old Swedish word *flinta*, meaning splinter of stone; or it may come from the Greek word *plinthos*, meaning brick. Flint is fine-grained and very hard, but when struck sharply, it will defoliate in characteristic conchoidal (shell-shaped) flakes on the face opposite the blow. This defoliation allows nodules of flint to be worked very precisely.

For thousands of years, flint technology was the mainstay of human survival skills.

▲ *Flint has the property of sparking when struck with steel, and thus it was a common firearm component in the late 17th century.*

Because flint sparks when struck, it was used to create fire. Our ancestors also used flint to make first simple and then very sophisticated and effective tools for a wide range of everyday needs. With the advent of gunpowder-based weapons in the sixteenth century, it was used in the firing mechanisms of guns until the mid-nineteenth century. Today, flint is used primarily as a building material in areas where it is commonly found, such as southern England. It is also used in road construction, and as an abrasive.

Because the shape of a flint nodule resembles bone, in ancient times it naturally became associated with the spirits of the Earth, the fairy folk, and ancestral spirits.

SPIRITUAL AND HEALING PROPERTIES

Flint helps the body to repair itself at every level, and also helps with the assimilation of nutrients. It has been used in many cultures as protection against negative influences, which it is said to absorb. It is also thought to improve self-confidence, and to help provide a strong sense of connection and belonging in relation to other people and the world in general.

This hard stone strengthens all of the subtle systems of the body, but focuses most at the level of the solar plexus chakra, imbuing confidence, personal power, and assimilation of information on all levels.

DIVINATORY INTERPRETATION

Flint is the stone of invention and innovation. In its natural formation, it is just a lump of rock, but with a bit of work, it can be transformed into a precise tool. In a positive placement, flint shows strength and ingenuity. However, in a difficult position, it may suggest conflict and negative influences. If this is the case, then the positive qualities of flint will help you escape from the aggression you are facing. It is usually within the conflict itself that the resolution can be found. Don't look elsewhere: examine the flashpoints—the sparks that have ignited the trouble—and learn to control them so that they can work to everyone's advantage. Remember that a fire can burn down a house, but it can also cook a meal. Use your skills to mold the situation constructively.

▼ *Found in many regions of the world, prehistoric flint arrowheads can tell us a great deal about how our ancestors lived and about their level of sophistication.*

SUGGESTED READINGS

Flint in center/First House
You need to appear strong, but at the same time, open to new ideas.

Flint in southeast/Second House
Have faith in your own strength and resolve.

Flint in east/Third House
Your ideas may seem out of step with those around you, but you are right.

Flint in north/Fourth House
Reassess your resources and assets and create a more secure base.

Flint in west/Fifth House
Be on the lookout for new experiences or hobbies.

Flint in Sixth House
Be willing to give others a helping hand in their quest for a new start.

Flint in southwest/Seventh House
Look to the root of any disagreements before trying to settle differences.

Flint in Eighth House
Unexpected events may seem to create havoc, but will have positive outcomes.

Flint in northeast/Ninth House
Trust your intuition to guide you to the next stage of the current situation.

Flint in south/Tenth House
Dare to be different and to see the present situation through, staying focused on your target.

Flint in northwest/Eleventh House
New friends and a new social scene have their thrills, but they may be tiring you out.

Flint in Twelfth House
You may be restless for no apparent reason. Keeping busy may help.

Solar plexus chakra
Midway between navel and base of ribs

▲ *Crystals are placed on the solar plexus chakra.*

Personality

Practical and inventive, the flint personality may also appear to be unresponsive and rigid, but with the right stimulus, this personality will help out whenever possible.

Energy

Strong, innovative, resourceful.

Amazonite

Amazonite is a variety of feldspar, the most common mineral within the Earth's crust.

Amazonite

Color: blue-green, with lighter striations

Hardness: 6–6.5

Composition: $KAISi_3O_8$ (potassium aluminosilicate)

Qualities: calming, communicative

Main chakras: throat, heart

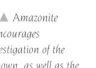

▲ *Amazonite encourages investigation of the unknown, as well as the reinterpretation of information in new and more relevant ways.*

Feldspar is a complex family of related minerals that includes many colorful and useful stones. Amazonite is one of the most easily identified members of the feldspar family because of its characteristic blue-green color. The mineral name for amazonite is microcline. Amazonite crystals are easy to identify, forming flat, columnar prisms that are clearly bounded, substantial-looking, and often intergrown.

Amazonite derives its name from the Amazon River in South America, even though it is jade, not amazonite, that is found there. A popular semiprecious gemstone, amazonite is commonly used for cabochons and beads. It is easily identified by its mottled, streaky, or parallel lines of lighter and darker greens, caused by atoms of lead within the crystal lattice.

MYTH AND HISTORY

The ancient Egyptians often used amazonite, or *uat*, as they called it, for carvings. Its color resembles turquoise—sometimes even emerald and jade. The colors of these stones were commonly associated with the afterlife, fertility, and protection from harm.

Amazonite is thought to have been among the stones in the Hebrew high priest's breastplate, as described in the book of Exodus.

SPIRITUAL AND HEALING PROPERTIES

The color of amazonite aligns it to the heart and throat chakras. It is a calming stone

▼ *Precious metals and gemstones can often be found deposited along the length of great rivers such as the Amazon. These materials require no elaborate mining to recover—just patience and a good eye.*

that helps to balance and stabilize the nervous system. Communication, memory, and brain functions are all enhanced by amazonite.

Like many turquoise and green stones, amazonite has been used to stimulate psychic skills and subtle sensitivity. It is sometimes even able to rekindle awareness of events from the distant past, known as "far memory." The images and sensations arising from far memory often relate in some way to the current life circumstances of the individual experiencing them.

DIVINATORY INTERPRETATION

The energies of the heart and throat combine in this stone to positively affect personal expression and creativity. In a reading, amazonite is related to sharing points of view, standing up and being counted, and the exploration of new experiences.

Amazonite indicates an outgoing, expansive phase of life motivated by a sincere desire to understand and to learn.

SUGGESTED READINGS

Amazonite in center/First House
You need to appear open-minded and interested in all possibilities.

Amazonite in southeast/Second House
Financial factors are crucial to your current situation.

Amazonite in east/Third House
Communicate clearly and precisely what you feel and think.

Amazonite in north/Fourth House
The foundations need to be further strengthened in order to support any more expansion.

Amazonite in west/Fifth House
Try new hobbies or learn new skills in order to broaden your knowledge base and to provide yourself with greater options.

Amazonite in Sixth House
Keep an outward, big-picture outlook on work, even if the going is tough.

Amazonite in southwest/Seventh House
Use a buoyant and optimistic approach in any sort of relationship discussion, but always be truthful.

Amazonite in Eighth House
Obstacles will be highlighted so that you can deal with them easily.

Amazonite in northeast/Ninth House
Keep your options open until you find something that really suits you.

Amazonite in south/Tenth House
Be prepared to step away from your usual routine and toward new experiences.

Amazonite in northwest/Eleventh House
Your opinion is needed in social situations.

Amazonite in Twelfth House
Restlessness may be intense, and you may feel trapped. If you relax, it will pass quickly.

Throat chakra
Neck
Heart chakra
Center of breastbone in center of chest

▲ *Crystals are placed on the throat and heart chakras.*

It also seeks to clarify where the individual is in his or her life, and what his or her purpose is in the world. This stone suggests that this is the time to embark on projects or challenges long dreamed about but never tried, to expand our horizons, and to dare to be a little different.

Personality

The personality associated with amazonite is one of an inquisitive person, always investigating the unknown and interested in a wide range of subjects. The amazonite person is also a good communicator and an intellectual.

Energy

Outgoing, curious.

Aquamarine

Aquamarine is the precious, clear blue-green variety of the mineral beryl.

Aquamarine

Color: blue, blue-green

Hardness: 7.5–8

Composition:
$Be_3Al_2Si_6O_{18}$ (beryl)

Qualities: expressive, cleansing

Main chakra: throat

▼ *and* ▶ *In ancient times, the colors within aquamarine so closely resembled the colors of the sea that the stone quickly became associated with the deities of the sea.*

Like all beryls, aquamarine is found in pegmatites, and can grow into large, hexagonal crystals. Often, these crystals contain thin, parallel cavities of gas and water and, as with other beryls, inclusions of mica and iron oxides are common.

Aquamarine shows dichroism; that is, the rich blue color seen from some angles almost disappears when seen from others. This characteristic can help to identify the many imitations of this crystal. Iron atoms within the lattice are the source of aquamarine's blue color. Because most jewelers prefer very particular shades of blue crystals, the less popular shades can be inexpensive to acquire.

MYTH AND HISTORY

The color of aquamarine has connected it to the element of water, and to the sea in particular. From the third century BC, Greeks and Romans used the stone as a protective charm for overseas journeys, together with cameos carved with images of Poseidon, god of the sea, with his trident. Aquamarine was also a symbol of happiness and hope and, like emerald, was associated with love and friendship.

SPIRITUAL AND HEALING PROPERTIES

Aquamarine can provide a significant boost to the immune system. It has a cleansing action that, in combination with its ability to stimulate the thymus gland, can help clear infection from the body. It may, however, bring old symptoms to the surface before they are finally released.

The throat chakra is energized by this crystal, encouraging creative expression and communication skills. There is also an improvement in mood, with an increase in hopefulness, optimism, and inspiration.

DIVINATORY INTERPRETATION

Aquamarine is a sign of communication in a reading. The interpretation of the reading will depend on whether the stone is located in a favorable or a difficult position. In a favorable position, this stone suggests companionship, conviviality, and a sharing of joy and optimism with loved ones. When surrounded by difficult energies, however, aquamarine may suggest that thoughtless gossip or the spreading of lies is causing problems. It may also indicate deception. Like imitations of the stone itself, this sort of behavior will become clear if you patiently examine the situation from many different angles. It is important, though, not to become too emotionally involved—in other words, keep your cool. In some positions, aquamarine may also suggest travel over water.

SUGGESTED READINGS

Aquamarine in center/First House
Be willing to offer companionship and support.

Aquamarine in southeast/Second House
Examine your own motivations before you blame others.

Aquamarine in east/Third House
Circumstances may require that you spend a lot of time talking.

Aquamarine in north/Fourth House
Do not ignore those at home in favor of a busy social life.

Aquamarine in west/Fifth House
Get out there and have some fun with friends.

Aquamarine in Sixth House
Do not take your work too seriously. Help others to keep the atmosphere light.

Aquamarine in southwest/Seventh House
There may be celebrations with close friends in your near future.

Aquamarine in Eighth House
Others really need you to be around to support them at this time.

Aquamarine in northeast/Ninth House
Travel over water for leisure purposes may be in your future.

Aquamarine in south/Tenth House
Insure that your plans include everyone who wants to join you.

Aquamarine in northwest/Eleventh House
Gossip may be clouding relationships with friends or other groups of people.

Aquamarine in Twelfth House
Take a few steps back so that you can see what is really going on.

Throat chakra
Neck

▲ *Crystals are placed on the throat chakra.*

◀ *The invigorating effects of the sea upon human beings has been noted for centuries. Similarly stimulating effects are attributed to the aquamarine crystal.*

Personality

Aquamarine represents a friendly, supportive, talkative person who is full of stories and ideas. This person might be connected to the sea or to seafaring in some way.

Energy

Companionable, convivial.

Celestite

Celestite is a soft crystal with a wonderful sky-blue translucence and powerful energies.

Celestite

Color: sky blue, gray, clear

Hardness: 3–3.5

Composition: $SrSO_4$ (strontium sulfate)

Qualities: light, meditative, spacious

Main chakras: throat, brow, crown

Celestite forms in hydrothermal veins, as well as in sedimentary and igneous rock. It usually forms as a result of volcanic activity, especially near the sea, in tabular or columnar crystals, often with a rhombohedral cross section. The most common coloration is a rich, transparent blue.

MYTH AND HISTORY

Celestite, also called celestine, derives its name from the Latin word *caelestis,* meaning heavenly, referring to the fine blue of its crystals. In India, it traditionally served a religious function; priests in Bengal would throw celestite powder onto fires to produce a vivid crimson flame. Nowadays, this igniting property—caused by the element strontium—is widely used industrially to make flares, fireworks, and tracer bullets. It is also used in some types of food processing, as well as in the making of glass and ceramics.

SPIRITUAL AND HEALING PROPERTIES

Celestite has remarkable relaxing and uplifting abilities. It can help to relieve feelings of sadness, heaviness, or desperation. This stone can bring about a calm, joyous state, where the subtle realms and finer levels of reality seem to be more easily accessible. All of these qualities make celestite a valuable stone for meditation and intuitive frames of mind. This crystal can also help to relieve any imbalances in the area of the throat chakra, affecting communication, expression, and acceptance. The crown and brow chakras are also stimulated by this crystal.

DIVINATORY INTERPRETATION

In a reading, celestite indicates the presence of spiritual influences. These influences may take the form of coincidences, lucky breaks, unexpected meetings, or simply of time spent in a pleasant, dreamy state.

Celestite can suggest the lifting of a heavy mood, the improvement of difficult circumstances, and the ability to see beyond problems. A safe, nurturing space is shown that will help recuperation and will reestablish a balanced calm once more. One must be cautious when this stone appears, however, not to sink too deeply into any otherworldly, dreamy reverie. Heightened states of awareness must always be grounded into everyday reality if they are to be of value.

In a negative placement, celestite might indicate an escape from reality into a fantasy world if other stones nearby show a lack of practical energy.

▲▶ *Whenever we watch a fireworks display, we*
▼ *are witnessing the combustion of many different materials, each one showing a different brilliant color. Celestite is typically the source of the deep red displays.*

SUGGESTED READINGS

Celestite in center/First House
Make a special effort to remain focused on matters around you.

Celestite in southeast/Second House
Avoid making any crucial decisions until you can see the situation more clearly.

Celestite in east/Third House
Unexpected meetings could prove to be very beneficial.

Celestite in north/Fourth House
Make your home a peaceful haven for visitors.

Celestite in west/Fifth House
Romantic encounters and other chance meetings are likely at this time.

Celestite in Sixth House
It may be difficult to focus on practicalities at the moment.

Celestite in southwest/Seventh House
Your dream of a perfect romantic partner is preventing you from seeing what you already have.

Celestite in Eighth House
There will be unexpected alterations to your plans.

Celestite in northeast/Ninth House
Wise words from others should be heeded.

Celestite in south/Tenth House
Your dreams and wishes will help keep you focused on the goal.

Celestite in northwest/Eleventh House
Take time to be with others of similar philosophical backgrounds.

Celestite in Twelfth House
You need to rest and recuperate. Leave the world behind for a while.

Crown chakra
Top of the head
Brow chakra
Center of forehead
Throat chakra
Neck

▲ *Crystals are placed on the crown, brow, and throat chakras.*

Personality

A celestite personality will tend to be in a world of their own: dreamy and contemplative, perhaps a little distant, and completely removed from everyday preoccupations.

Energy

Otherworldly, dreamy, spiritual.

Turquoise

In many ancient cultures, turquoise was used as an amulet for protection and was a symbol of wealth.

Turquoise

Color: light blue, blue-green, green

Hardness: 5–6

Composition: $CuAl_6(PO_4)_4(OH)_8 \cdot 4\text{-}5H_2O$ (hydrated phosphate of aluminum and copper)

Qualities: strengthening, supportive

Main chakra: throat

Turquoise is created when water comes into contact with, and acts upon, a combination of copper and aluminum minerals. The resulting crystals are very small, and usually occur in massive form or granules. The stone's blue color derives from its copper content, whereas the green tones are due to impurities. It is easy to identify turquoise from different areas by appearance—even individual mines can often be recognized from the appearance of the stones.

Turquoise is very porous, and easily absorbs dirt and oils. Heat and sunlight will often change its color. To stabilize its color and reduce its porousness, turquoise is often impregnated with a wax or resin.

MYTH AND HISTORY

Turquoise was mined by the ancient Egyptians in the Sinai Peninsula, near the Red Sea. It was also mined in Persia. The Ottoman Turks valued the stone and, despite some turquoise being found in Anatolia, they continued the often difficult trading process with the tribes controlling the mining operations. This demand for turquoise made it an expensive and valuable commodity. It entered the European markets via Turkey, and thus, from the thirteenth century onward, it became known as "turquoise," the Turkish stone.

In Persia, turquoise was used to protect men and horses from falls and injuries. A thirteenth-century Persian book on the virtues of stones says, "Whoever owns the true turquoise set in gold will not injure any of his limbs when he falls, whether he be riding or walking, so long as he has the stone with him."

Historically, turquoise was a popular stone in Europe, and was typically worn by men as a gemstone set in rings. The Native

▼ *In this pendant from Tibet, turquoise is set in gold, along with lapis lazuli and rubies.*

American peoples—particularly in the southwestern states, where turquoise is found—valued the stone as a hunting aid. They also used it as a tool for healers and shamans, and for protection against harm. The Aztecs and Mayas used turquoise as an offering to the gods, and in China and Tibet, turquoise has long been worn as a protective amulet, and in a jewelry format as a sign of wealth.

SPIRITUAL AND HEALING PROPERTIES

As a blue stone with a hint of green, turquoise works naturally at the level of the heart and throat chakras. In particular, it stimulates the subtle energies of the thymus gland, midway between the heart and throat, an area which plays an important part in the body's immune system. Turquoise also acts as a general strengthener for all systems of the body, and offers protection from harm by ensuring a high level of energy function. The effects of environmental pollution and negativity are reduced and, as with many green- and turquoise-colored stones, psychic sensitivity and connection with the spirit world are enhanced.

DIVINATORY INTERPRETATION

Turquoise appearing in a reading suggests the need to take precautions for personal safety. Be wary, be alert, and be prepared to deal with whatever unforeseen difficulties may arise. This is not an indication of danger; it is simply a warning that the situation requires care and extra attention.

In a positive placement, turquoise can show that everything is working in harmony; all factors are balanced, and there is a general optimistic atmosphere. Turquoise also suggests that, in order for things to work at optimum levels, you must communicate your feelings and preferences. Where health is an issue, turquoise may indicate a need to monitor the level of present environmental stresses, including pollution, electromagnetic radiation, noise, as well as negative emotions.

SUGGESTED READINGS

Turquoise in center/First House
Be wary and cautious in the ways in which you respond to people and events.

Throat chakra Neck

Turquoise in southeast/Second House
Your energy levels may not be at their best, so learn to pace yourself.

Turquoise in east/Third House
Say what you mean to say, not what someone else wants to hear.

Turquoise in north/Fourth House
Double-check your security at home. Emotional boundaries may need some attention.

Turquoise in west/Fifth House
Allow your instincts to guide your creative activities.

Turquoise in Sixth House
Pay attention to your health. Eat well, and don't overwork yourself.

Turquoise in southwest/Seventh House
Do not ignore your own wishes when making decisions.

Turquoise in Eighth House
Be careful not to exceed your budget at the moment.

Turquoise in northeast/Ninth House
Teachers and guides can help you clarify your thoughts and feelings.

Turquoise in south/Tenth House
Make sure you have a secure fallback position.

Turquoise in northwest/Eleventh House
Friends can help you to regain your sense of security.

Turquoise in Twelfth House
Take time to explore the spiritual aspects of your life.

▲ *Crystals are placed on the throat chakra.*

▲◄ *In this Tibetan brooch, the powers of the heavens, represented by turquoise, are united with those of the earth, represented by rubies.*

Personality

Self-contained and assured, the turquoise personality is skilled in the physical world, but also has a firm foundation in the spirit world. He or she is likely a teacher, healer, or guide.

Energy

Immune, protective.

Sapphire

Sapphire is the blue variety of the mineral corundum, one of the hardest of all stones.

Sapphire

Color: blue, blue-violet, yellow, white

Hardness: 9

Composition: Al_2O_3 + Fe & Ti (aluminum oxide)

Properties: encouraging spiritually aware, regulating

Main chakras: brow, crown

▼ *Sapphires for the gem industry are valued by their richness of color and lack of internal flaws.*

Sapphire is the name given to all types of corundum except for the red variety, which is called ruby. Although the blue stone is the most well known and highly prized, sapphires also occur in yellow and white, although these colors often turn blue upon heating. The rich coloration of blue sapphire is caused by impurities of iron and titanium oxides within the crystal matrix.

This crystal is characteristically barrel-shaped, with six sides. It is found in metamorphic rocks that have been subjected to great heat and pressure, and also in alluvial deposits, where the bedrock has eroded.

MYTH AND HISTORY

Sapphire has always been one of the most precious of gemstones, both for its color and its hardness, second only to diamond. India and Sri Lanka both have many famous deposits that have been actively mined for many thousands of years.

It is said that, traditionally, royalty wore sapphires to protect themselves from harm and from the envy of others. The rich blue of the stone was thought to suggest a pure sky that encouraged divine favor and spiritual blessings. Sapphire was also thought to enable seers to better understand the most obscure and difficult of oracles. The stone was used as well to influence all sorts of spirits, and so became a favorite of witches and magicians.

Star sapphire is the most auspicious type of sapphire. The star formation occurs in the transparent stones, where microscopic intergrown crystals reflect the light

▼ *Explorer Richard Burton owned a large star sapphire and claimed it brought prompt service wherever he went.*

on the polished dome of a cabochon cut in a perfect six-pointed star. The great explorer Sir Richard Burton had a star sapphire with him always—not just for luck, but also as a way to impress others to do his bidding. In medieval Germany, star sapphire was known as the "victory stone," and was considered a powerful protection from the evil eye.

SPIRITUAL AND HEALING PROPERTIES

Sapphire has a calming and regulating effect on many systems of the body. Wherever there is overactivity and a buildup of tension, sapphire brings a cool relaxation. Anxiety eases, there is a smoother flow of communication and personal expression, and the higher mind is stimulated, enabling an improved experiencing of the subtle states of perception.

Star sapphire emphasizes the spiritual energies of the mineral, aiding clairvoyance and visionary experience. All types and colors of sapphire can be useful aids to meditation.

DIVINATORY INTERPRETATION

Sapphire in a cast indicates the need for great precision and clarity in all actions. If emotions are troubled, this stone suggests the need for reestablishing a collected, cool, and considered state. It is important to understand the motivations of those around you, and to be able to properly interpret what people are saying and why.

In areas where problems exist, sapphire shows a relaxed, harmonious, and rejuvenating environment. However, acting from a purely personal viewpoint and in response to one's own emotional states is to be

avoided in the areas where sapphire falls in a reading. Keep your wits about you and pay attention to clues that may inform you as to the true feelings of the people you are dealing with. In keeping your mind attentive, you may notice, too, how you are reacting to others. You might be surprised at how easy it is for your immediate emotional responses to confuse and muddy the situation.

SUGGESTED READINGS

Sapphire in center/First House
People expect you to be able to see all aspects of the situation.

Sapphire in southeast/Second House
Clarify your motives before taking any action.

Sapphire in east/Third House
Put your ideas across clearly, precisely, and with minimal fuss.

Sapphire in north/Fourth House
Make an effort to finish jobs and projects at home.

Sapphire in west/Fifth House
Take up challenges and start developing and honing new skills.

Sapphire in Sixth House
Clarity and precision are needed in your work.

Sapphire in southwest/Seventh House
Take yourself and your partner to a peaceful, natural setting.

Sapphire in Eighth House
See if you can put your resources to better use.

Sapphire in northeast/Ninth House
Focus your energy on a few specific areas rather than on broad bands of interest.

Sapphire in south/Tenth House
You have the opportunity to relaunch or expand your role.

Sapphire in northwest/Eleventh House
Be choosy about your social activities—don't commit yourself to too many events.

Sapphire in Twelfth House
If you want to get some peace, you must detach yourself from the emotions of those around you.

Crown chakra Top of the head
Brow chakra Center of forehead

▲ *Crystals are placed on the crown and brow chakras.*

Personality
Sapphire represents a very observant person who likes to stand back and watch rather than take part in the action. This person also works with spiritual and psychic energies as a matter of course—not for the glamour of it.

Energy
Expansive, precise, understanding.

Rock Crystal

Rock crystal is the common name for transparent, clear quartz. This stone has been used for thousands of years for both healing and prophecy.

Rock crystal

Color: transparent, clear

Hardness: 7

Composition: SiO_2

Qualities: clear, orderly, calm

Main chakras: all

Clear quartz is the pure form of the mineral silicon dioxide. It is free of any impurity in the crystal lattice that might create color, and forms long, hexagonal crystals that meet at a single point. It originates in volcanic rock, where silica-rich solutions cool and crystallize within cracks and cavities. A hard-wearing stone, quartz finds its way via eroded material into sedimentary layers, rivers, and seabeds. The great majority of beach pebbles are quartz varieties, and sand itself is mostly silicate minerals.

MYTH AND HISTORY

In ancient Greece, there were some who believed that clear quartz was ice that had frozen so completely that it would never melt again, *crystallos* being the Greek word for ice. Other ancient peoples associated quartz with the sky worlds, and saw it as fragments from the heavenly realms.

Historically, quartz was universally used as a tool for divination, scrying, and healing—particularly for divining the causes of disease and for the removal of imbalances caused by the spirits. Clear quartz was one of the favorite materials for fashioning mirrors and spheres for scrying. It was also ground into lenses and cut to make goblets and bowls for ritual purposes. Among the most famous of quartz carvings are the crystal skulls attributed to the ancient cultures of South and Central America.

In the development of modern technology, quartz crystal has been vital. For example, tons of Brazilian quartz was mined during World War II for radio sets. Quartz is also widely used as a component in precision equipment, although laboratory-made crystals are now the main source for the industry.

SPIRITUAL AND HEALING PROPERTIES

Rock crystal has an organizing and harmonizing effect on all parts of the body with which it comes into contact. It can be especially calming, and will quickly restore a more balanced energy. It also helps to dissipate all areas of imbalance and negativity,

▲ *Many instances of healing and otherworldly communications have been attributed to ancient crystal skulls.*

and establishes calmness and clarity in the mind, making it a useful stone for meditation and healing techniques.

Rock crystal tends to amplify the qualities of stones nearby. It will also amplify positive frequencies of energy, making coherent, life-enhancing energies more effective, while reducing or neutralizing chaotic or unharmonious ones.

DIVINATORY INTERPRETATION

Rock crystal acts as a focus for solidity and organization in a reading, and brings clarity and understanding. It helps keep necessary information out in the open, and ensures that nothing is withheld or disguised. All activities will tend to be productive and helpful in the areas where rock crystal falls. Only when the questioner is planning some sort of subterfuge or secret dealings will this stone indicate a failure of plans; this is because everything will become transparent and obvious to all involved.

SUGGESTED READINGS

Crown chakra
Top of the head

Brow chakra
Center of forehead

Throat chakra
Neck

Heart chakra
Center of breastbone
in center of chest

Solar plexus chakra
Midway between
navel and base of ribs

Sacral chakra
Midway between
navel and pubic bone

Base (root) chakra
Base of spine
(perineum)

▲ *Crystals are placed on all of the chakras.*

Rock crystal in center/First House
Be yourself. Let others see how you really feel.

Rock crystal in southeast/Second House
Doubts need to be resolved if you are going to make progress.

Rock crystal in east/Third House
Explain things carefully to others, repeating yourself until you are sure they understand.

Rock crystal in north/Fourth House
Issues surrounding the home and family cannot be ignored any longer.

Rock crystal in west/Fifth House
It is not a good time to take risks or to gamble. Stick with what you are sure of.

Rock crystal in Sixth House
This is an ideal time to resolve difficulties in the workplace.

Rock crystal in southwest/Seventh House
Pretense should have no place in your relationships or partnerships.

Rock crystal in Eighth House
Financial dealings need to be honest and transparent.

Rock crystal in northeast/Ninth House
Your perception of current circumstances is particularly clear at the moment—be guided by it.

Rock crystal in south/Tenth House
Your plans need to be clear and open to scrutiny by others.

Rock crystal in northwest/Eleventh House
A frank exchange of ideas may help to clarify problems or disagreements.

Rock crystal in Twelfth House
You need to be sure that you are not working to a hidden agenda that is clouding the issue.

◀ *Before the advent of electric light, rock crystal was often used to reflect candlelight in candelabra and table fountains. This rock crystal and gold table fountain was made specially for the Medici family.*

Personality

Rock crystal indicates a bright, organized, orderly individual with a calm, clear mind and a positive emotional outlook.

Energy

Clear, transparent, coherent.

Selenite

Selenite is named for the ancient Greek goddess of the moon, Selene, because of its gentle white luster.

Selenite

Color: transparent, white, gray

Hardness: 2

Composition: $CaSO_4 2H_2O$ (gypsum variety)

Qualities: energy-shifting, expansive

Main chakras: crown, sacral

Selenite is the transparent, gem-quality variety of the common mineral gypsum. It forms long, blade-like crystals made up of parallel sheets of rock. Gypsum is extremely soft and can be easily scratched with a fingernail. It is formed from the evaporation of saltwater lakes and the ancient seas.

MYTH AND HISTORY

The extreme delicacy of selenite severely limits its use—the stone has a high water content, and exposure to heat or a change of humidity can bend the crystals. If left in water for too long, selenite can easily separate into thin leaves.

The Greek sculptor Lysippus is said to have been the first to use gypsum as a casting material. Today, its use for casting is widespread, and in this context, it is commonly known as plaster of Paris. Plaster of Paris is simply gypsum heated to about 7,230°F (4,000°C), to drive out the water (once water is reintroduced, the material recrystallizes). When heated above this temperature, gypsum is suitable for making paint bulkers and cement. The fine, granular, massive form of gypsum is known as alabaster, and has long been an important sculpting material.

SPIRITUAL AND HEALING PROPERTIES

Selenite is one of the best stones with which to bring about a rapid shift of energy. It can quickly disperse accumulations of negativity in the aura, and will remove blockages and stagnant energy from the body. Selenite also brings flexibility, spiritual insight, and creativity. It can be relaxing and eases bodily tension.

◀ *In prehistoric times, alabaster was often used for carving statues, particularly in Middle Eastern and Eastern Mediterranean regions.*

▶ *A soft, fragile material, plaster of Paris (gypsum) is nevertheless able to create a substance strong enough to keep broken bones in place until they knit together.*

DIVINATORY INTERPRETATION

When it appears in a reading, selenite suggests that the situation is extremely delicate. On the surface, things may appear to be fine, with nothing apparently amiss. In reality, however, the situation is inherently unstable. This doesn't necessarily mean that things are going to get worse, but it does mean that some sort of change lies ahead. As selenite is associated with the moon, and the cycle of the moon is around twenty-eight days, it may be that change will occur within a month of the day of the reading. Precisely what that change will be may be indicated by the fall of other stones, or by the area occupied by selenite in the cast.

Selenite will indicate problems in a reading only if the questioner is unwilling to face change in the area of his or her life to which it relates. In a situation that is difficult or blocked, selenite provides instant relief by allowing the energies involved to move once more. Once circumstances begin to change, there will be a rapid alteration in all lives involved.

Selenite in a personal placement suggests that the questioner move very carefully, as he or she is extremely vulnerable. Negative emotions such as anger and fear

should be allowed to dissolve before they precipitate unexpected and unwelcome responses. In partnerships, selenite can indicate the need to maintain sympathetic and open conditions. Any change now may result in one stress too many and lead to a parting of ways.

SUGGESTED READINGS

Selenite in center/First House
Be flexible and philosophical, as there is little you can do about the situation.

Selenite in southeast/Second House
Trying to keep to a routine is likely to be pointless at the moment.

Selenite in east/Third House
Other people's reactions show you how delicate circumstances are at present.

Selenite in north/Fourth House
You may be feeling sorry for yourself, but this will pass.

Selenite in west/Fifth House
Soft music and gentle relaxation in beautiful surroundings are needed now.

Selenite in Sixth House
Your health may not be at its most robust, so take it easy for a while.

Selenite in southwest/Seventh House
Be sympathetic to those close to you—listen but do not react.

Selenite in Eighth House
Others' emotions are deeply connected here, so be prepared for sudden changes.

Selenite in northeast/Ninth House
Life is likely to feel like a rollercoaster ride, so just let go and flow with it.

Selenite in south/Tenth House
The current situation is too unstable to make plans for the future.

Selenite in northwest/Eleventh House
For the next few weeks, group situations could be very finely balanced, so respond with care.

Selenite in Twelfth House
Keep your feet on the ground and try not to get carried away with whims and illusions.

Crown chakra
Top of the head

Sacral chakra
Midway between navel and pubic bone

▲ *Crystals are placed on the crown and sacral chakras.*

Personality

Watch out for the selenite personality. They may appear attractive and friendly, but in reality they can be unreliable and unstable.

Energy

Fluctuating, vulnerable.

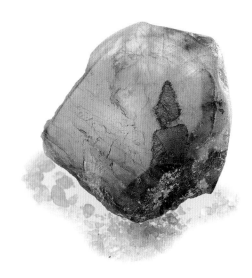

Labradorite

Labradorite is a chameleonlike stone, ranging from the dullest of grays to peacock iridescence as it catches the light.

Labradorite

Color: gray with blue, green, and orange iridescence.

Hardness: 6

Composition:
$(Na, Ca)Al_{1-2}Si_{3-2}2O_8$
(plagioclase feldspar)

Qualities: camouflage, energy-shifting

Main chakras: all

Labradorite is a special variety of feldspar. Large areas of the stone are exceptionally iridescent. The color is caused by light refracting from microscopic crystals of various dark minerals, usually ilmenite, hematite, and magnetite, and from fine intergrowths of labradorite crystals. It is common in massive form; crystals are rare and small. Labradorite is found in both igneous and metamorphic conditions.

MYTH AND HISTORY

In the late eighteenth century, a missionary exploring the shores of Labrador found boulders of this strange mineral. Soon after this initial identification, labradorite was found in Finland and the Ukraine, although Labrador remained the primary source for gem-quality stone. The beauty of the stone ensured that it quickly became favored for carving ornaments and jewelry.

▲ *Wearing labradorite can provide a boost of energy for those who tire easily in the company of others.*

SPIRITUAL AND HEALING PROPERTIES

Labradorite allows complete polarity shifts to occur. Just as different colors appear on the surface of the stone, so the stone helps many different levels of energy and awareness to be accessed by the individual. Because of this quality, it can be an ideal stone to help discover new solutions and reveal new opportunities in life.

The ability of labradorite to instigate rapid frequency shifts enables the body chakras to move easily between dimensional states. This can remove blockages rapidly, and can help to establish new patterns of behavior that are more appropriate to the individual.

Labradorite is a very useful stone for energy protection, as the ever-changing colors prevent negativity from attaching to any one place. It also prevents energy drainage and reduces co-dependency.

DIVINATORY INTERPRETATION

Labradorite indicates surprise, transformation, and transmutation. It brings a sudden change of circumstances that enables a stagnant situation to revive and move on in a positive way. New opportunities will arise, a variety of choices will present themselves, and life will suddenly become full of excitement and opportunity.

The lesson of this stone is never to make assumptions. In relationships, labradorite can indicate the need to look carefully at what you have; taking the situation for granted creates boredom and a stifling routine. Do something unnecessary, unexpected, and generous. Show your appreciation for your partner.

If labradorite is found in a position of health, it may show the need to monitor personal energies. Do you always feel drained in the presence of some people, and do those people feel better for being with you? If you work with many people all day long, or are in a stressful occupation where emotions can be strongly broadcast, labradorite can indicate that your energy is not being replenished sufficiently, and that you are accumulating stress.

SUGGESTED READINGS

Labradorite in center/First House
You need to stand firm and not be swayed by the dominant view.

Labradorite in southeast/Second House
Look at ways of eliminating waste and unecessary pressures from your life.

Labradorite in east/Third House
Choices should be intuitive rather than based on intellectual thought.

Labradorite in north/Fourth House
Consider rearranging things at home to create a sense of more space and light.

Labradorite in west/Fifth House
Try to do more outdoors, in a natural environment.

Labradorite in Sixth House
Look after your health, especially if demanding people surround you.

Labradorite in southwest/Seventh House
Make the most of your relationships and partnerships.

Labradorite in Eighth House
It is time to transform or release old situations.

Labradorite in northeast/Ninth House
Unexpected opportunities may change your view of the situation.

Labradorite in south/Tenth House
Old plans and ideas may once again be relevant, and may need to be relaunched.

Labradorite in northwest/Eleventh House
Don't take your friends for granted. Find a way to show your appreciation for them.

Labradorite in Twelfth House
Quiet times will help you regain your energy and enthusiasm.

Crown chakra
Top of the head

Brow chakra
Center of forehead

Throat chakra
Neck

Heart chakra
Center of breastbone in center of chest

Solar plexus chakra
Midway between navel and base of ribs

Sacral chakra
Midway between navel and pubic bone

Base (root) chakra
Base of spine (perineum)

▲ *Crystals are placed on all of the chakras.*

◀ *Like the metamorphosis of a caterpillar into a butterfly, labradorite can transform stagnant, dull energies into fresh, vibrant ones, and can signal the advent of brand new beginnings.*

Personality

This crystal represents a seemingly dull, boring person who, as you suddenly discover, has always had—unbeknownst to you—a much more exciting life than you have!

Energy

Transformative, surprising, unexpected.

Rhodonite

The deep salmon-pink coloration of rhodonite has made it a popular carving stone.

Rhodonite

Color: pink, dark pink with veins of black or brown

Hardness: 5.5–6.5

Composition: $CaMn_4(SiO_3)_5$ (silicate of manganese and calcium)

Qualities: empowering, practical, compassionate

Main chakra: heart

▶ *Named for the rose, a classic symbol of romance, rhodonite is particularly beneficial in the realm of romantic relationships, as it encourages balance, solidity, trust, and understanding.*

Rhodonite forms in metamorphic rocks such as marble, where there is a high manganese content. It mainly occurs in evenly grained massive form which, together with its coloration, make it ideal as a carving material. Crystals are rare, and are table-top-shaped when they appear. Rhodonite is very often characterized by dark veins of manganese oxides, which increase its value as a gemstone. It is usually translucent, though transparent forms do occur.

MYTH AND HISTORY

Identified only in 1819, rhodonite takes its name from the Greek word *rhodon*, meaning "rose." Sources of quality crystals include Brazil, Finland, Japan, and Mexico. The mineral is often used to make ornamental figures and large *objets d'art*; it is also used in ceramic glazes and artists' pigments.

SPIRITUAL AND HEALING PROPERTIES

The color of rhodonite helps bring balance to the heart chakra, ensuring a realistic and practical approach to the emotions and to emotional responses. The darker colors within the pink hue bring a stabilizing and grounding energy that can be useful for alleviating negative states such as confusion and anxiety. The magenta tones boost confidence and motivation.

Rhodonite is also thought to be useful for those who work with mantras and the subtle qualities of sound, as it increases the practitioner's sensitivity.

DIVINATORY INTERPRETATION

Rhodonite appearing in a reading warns that the questioner must be practical in any emotional decision-making. In other words, don't get carried away with what might be. Focus on the present moment and what is possible and safe to achieve. A failure to be practical now will only add to any confusion or anxiety.

In a positive placement, rhodonite shows that emotional relationships have a firm, solid basis, resting on mutual appreciation and understanding. Where it appears in a placement related directly to the questioner, issues linked to self-esteem and self-confidence need to be addressed. There may be a lack of self-love, or perhaps too much self-confidence. Either extreme will present difficulties in acting appropriately in the situation at hand. In either of these circumstances, balance can be achieved by recognizing and removing emotional baggage from the past that is influencing present relationships. A good way forward is to see if there are any repeating patterns occurring in your relationships. Are the same types of personalities involved? Do the same sorts of scenarios keep reappearing? Although breaking a pattern risks letting the unexpected occur, it is the only way forward in a negative cycle.

SUGGESTED READINGS

Rhodonite in center/First House
Let others see you as having learned from past mistakes.

Rhodonite in southeast/Second House
Poor management of personal resources needs to be addressed if security is desired.

Heart Chakra
Center of breastbone in center of chest

Rhodonite in east/Third House
You may need to tone down personal feelings when explaining to others where problems lie.

Rhodonite in north/Fourth House
Look for old emotional patterns that keep recurring and take steps to deal with them.

▲ *Crystals are placed on the heart chakra.*

Rhodonite in west/Fifth House
Indulge yourself in a luxury you seldom have the chance to enjoy.

Rhodonite in Sixth House
Prominent health issues may need a complementary approach—try crystal healing, acupuncture, or shiatsu.

Rhodonite in southwest/Seventh House
Emotional vulnerability in close relationships needs to be examined and understood.

Rhodonite in Eighth House
Take time out to support others who are having difficulties, but only if you can offer them practical suggestions.

Rhodonite in northeast/Ninth House
Tackle new projects or ideas enthusiastically, but stay focused on the practical issues.

Rhodonite in south/Tenth House
Be pleased with yourself for what you have managed to achieve.

Rhodonite in northwest/Eleventh House
Help others to feel confident in themselves and their skills.

Rhodonite in Twelfth House
Be open to the problems of other people, but don't get emotionally involved.

◄ *Sound, particularly music, has a direct effect upon both the emotions and the heart chakra. Rhodonite can help balance these areas, thereby increasing emotional stability.*

Personality

This crystal is characterized by either a very grounded, passionate, down-to-earth person, or by one who lacks assuredness and self-confidence.

Energy

Practical, motivated, insecure.

Rose Quartz

Rose quartz is considered to be one of the most powerful stones for emotional healing.

Rose quartz

Color: pink, rose, peach, violet-pink

Hardness: 7

Composition: SiO_2

Qualities: emotional release, calming

Main chakra: heart

▶ *Rough pieces of rose quartz are often just as attractive as rare, translucent, gem-quality specimens.*

Rose quartz is an uncommon variety of quartz. It occurs primarily in massive, microcrystalline form; only very recently have larger crystals been found in some Brazilian mines. Transparent, gem-quality rose quartz is also rare—most specimens are cloudy. Rose quartz is very brittle and often contains many fractures. Because of its high value, it is used almost exclusively for jewelry and ornamentation. The pink color is thought to derive from titanium or manganese oxides.

MYTH AND HISTORY

Rose quartz was highly valued in the classical world both for its decorative qualities and its healing properties. The Romans imported rose quartz from mines in Sri Lanka, India, and even Russia. Carved intaglios and cameos, as well as personal seal rings, still exist from this period.

SPIRITUAL AND HEALING PROPERTIES

Rose quartz is an effective stone for reducing all aggravating or aggressive conditions. It encourages better understanding and increases self-worth. Further, it helps to neutralize the damage caused by poor self-image and a build-up of emotional stress, both of which can prevent effective healing. Placed close to the heart, large pieces of rose quartz can release stress and trauma rapidly. Sometimes this process can cause discomfort, and so care should be taken to balance the release with calming and stabilizing stones.

DIVINATORY INTERPRETATION

Rose quartz is the stone of relationships. It relates to friends, lovers, and those areas of our lives to which we devote a lot of emotional energy. Whatever we feel sustains us is represented by rose quartz. The position in which the stone falls in a reading shows not only where we are strongest, but also where we are the most sensitive.

In a difficult placement, rose quartz may show fissures in self-image and self-confidence. There may be problems with aggression or misunderstandings. In a positive placement, the stone will confirm a situation of support, friendship, emotional well-being, and love.

SUGGESTED READINGS

Rose quartz in center/First House
Be loving and supportive of those around you.

Rose quartz in southeast/Second House
A lack of self-confidence may be at the root of your current situation.

Rose quartz in east/Third House
Be sensitive when speaking to others.

Rose quartz in north/Fourth House
You need to focus on turning your home into a more loving and caring environment.

Rose quartz in west/Fifth House
Emotional times for new relationships and relationships with children are ahead.

Rose quartz in Sixth House
Be kind to yourself. Being overcritical and a perfectionist is causing you stress and anxiety.

Rose quartz in southwest/Seventh House
Accept those close to you for who and what they are

Rose quartz in Eighth House
You may be oversensitive to the moods of others, which leaves you feeling tired.

Rose quartz in northeast/Ninth House
Meeting up with friends more often will help boost your confidence.

Rose quartz in south/Tenth House
Be kind and open, but most of all be firm in your dealings with others.

Rose quartz in northwest/Eleventh House
A misunderstanding may have caused problems with friends. Work out your differences.

Rose quartz in Twelfth House
Look closely at how you see yourself. You may find that you need to change your negative impressions.

Heart chakra Center of breastbone in center of chest

▲ Crystals are placed on the heart chakra.

◄ Rose quartz is particularly useful for balancing the energies in a relationship, especially where there is a lack of confidence or trust.

Personality

Rose quartz represents a person who is empathic, sympathetic, and supportive of other people's lives. Emotional expression is strong and forthright, with no hidden agendas or manipulation.

Energy

Emotional, loving, sensitive.

Rubellite in Lepidolite

The harmonious blend of these two minerals can help free us from the influences of the past.

Lepidolite

Color: gray-pink, purple-gray

Hardness: 2.5–4

Composition:
$K(Li,Al)_3(Si,Al)_4O_{10}(F,OH)_2$
(lithium mica)

Qualities: honest, forgiving

Main chakras: heart, crown

▲ *Because of the relative differences in hardness, this mineral combination cannot be used for carving or jewelry making.*

Rubellite is a red variety of tourmaline that often grows in the same environment as lepidolite. Lepidolite, also known as lithium mica, forms deep in the ground under igneous conditions. It grows in small, rough scales, and is commonly found as a massive aggregate with a beautiful purple-pink color. Like all mica, it has a very reflective surface, so the pink rock shimmers and glistens in its rough form. Lepidolite is a source of the rare metal lithium, which is used in the making of alloys and batteries.

MYTH AND HISTORY

When lepidolite contains the rare element rubidium, it can be used for geological dating. Although relatively soft and fragile, it is often worn as a gemstone, tumbled or polished into a cabochon to show its pearly luster and deep color to best advantage.

Rubellite often intergrows with lepidolite, showing as lengths of pink or red tourmaline throughout the rock. As with many other colored, transparent tourmalines, rubellite has a long history of being cut as a gemstone.

SPIRITUAL AND HEALING PROPERTIES

Rubellite is a fine balancer for the heart chakra, and can help energize and stabilize the emotions; it is calming in its paler varieties and more stimulating in its darker tones. Rubellite clears away the negativity associated with aggression, and helps to introduce more assertiveness where there is too much acceptance and passivity. Pink stones help to balance the creative aspects of the sacral chakra, where deep trauma tends to be stored.

Lepidolite is best known for its ability to reduce stress and soothe the emotions. With its purple and pink coloration, it produces the same calming effect as is achieved when amethyst and rose quartz are paired together. All aspects of self-esteem are strengthened, encouraging honest, open levels of communication.

When found unified as a single stone, rubellite in lepidolite is an ideal combination for clearing emotional debris from the past away from the aura and the heart.

DIVINATORY INTERPRETATION

Rubellite in lepidolite in a reading shows the influence of the past arising to affect events in the present. In a positive setting, it shows that the questioner is gathering the fruits of positive actions. Relaxation at the end of a long process of creativity is well deserved, and the questioner should sit back and enjoy the results.

When rubellite in lepidolite is surrounded by more difficult energies, it can show that the questioner may be feeling shame or guilt for some real or imagined occurrence. Alternatively, it may show that negativity is being directed at the questioner from those who feel that he or she is to blame for something.

Rubellite in lepidolite can also indicate feuds, grudges, or resentments held over considerable periods of time that sour relationships. The lesson of this blend of stones is that forgiveness and acceptance—together with the negative polarity of blame and resentment—stem from the self. Such emotions are simply a mirroring of our own problems with the world. If we act to release the hurt from ourselves, the process of reconciliation will spontaneously begin.

SUGGESTED READINGS

Rubellite in lepidolite in center/First House
You have a need to be seen to be at peace with yourself.

Rubellite in lepidolite in southeast/Second House
Judging yourself too harshly only damages you—give yourself the praise you deserve.

Rubellite in lepidolite in east/Third House
Ignore any gossip or idle chatter about yourself or about those around you.

Rubellite in lepidolite in north/Fourth House
Deep emotional problems within your family need to be brought to the surface.

Rubellite in lepidolite in west/Fifth House
You will attract love and attention only when you feel that you deserve it.

Rubellite in lepidolite in Sixth House
Make a specific effort to rest and relax to give your body time to heal.

Crown chakra
Top of the head

Heart chakra
Center of breastbone in center of chest

Rubellite in lepidolite in southwest/ Seventh House
It is time to settle disagreements or arguments in close relationships.

Rubellite in lepidolite in Eighth House
Allow resentment about old hurts to be released or dissolved.

Rubellite in lepidolite in northeast/Ninth House
Be careful not to blame others for missed opportunities or spoiled chances.

▲ *Crystals are placed on the crown and heart chakras.*

Rubellite in lepidolite in south/ Tenth House
Be aware that in your effort to reach your goals, you may have upset others.

Rubellite in lepidolite in northwest/Eleventh House
Don't let other people overlook your presence or opinions—stand up and be noticed.

Rubellite in lepidolite in Twelfth House
If you feel like a victim, resolve the issue in another way.

◄ *Rubellite in lepidolite can bring clarity and acceptance to troubled relationships.*

▲◄ *Lepidolite is an important source of lithium for batteries.*

Personality

Rubellite in lepidolite may suggest someone who is trapped in the past in some way, and cannot forget an event—either positive or traumatic in nature—that happened to them. Alternatively, it may represent someone who deals with history and the passage of time.

Energy

Accepting, reconciliatory.

Fluorite

Fluorite is one of the most attractive of all mineral forms, and has a wide range of industrial uses.

Fluorite

Color: purple, blue, green, yellow, clear

Hardness: 4

Composition: CaF_2 (calcium fluoride)

Qualities: inventive, innovative, coordinated

Main chakra: brow

▲ *Fluorite not only encourages the invention of new technologies—it can also be a key ingredient within them.*

Fluorite is a common mineral that forms when mineral veins come into contact with hot water. It is often found together with such minerals as silver, tin, and lead, and thus miners have been familiar with this mineral for many centuries. Fluorite appears in a wide range of colors. The cubic form of its crystals can result in striking clusters of stepped and pyramidal shapes.

MYTH AND HISTORY

The Romans imported fluorite from Iran (then known as Parthia) to make the famous murrhine vases. The Greeks also used fluorite as an ornamental stone. Because of its value, fluorite was widely imitated using special glass-making processes.

Fluorite takes its name from the Latin word *fluere*, meaning "to flow." It is so named because of its low melting temperature. In some areas of the world, miners called it the "ore flower."

In the early nineteenth century it was discovered that, when certain frequencies of light were shone upon the stone, it would emit light of a different color. This characteristic became known as "fluorescence."

Today, fluorite is a very important industrial mineral. It is the main source for the fluorine gas and hydrofluoric acid used to make steel, enamel, and glassware, and is also used in refrigerator coolants (chlorofluorocarbons, or CFCs), rocket technology, and nonstick coatings. It is used as a disinfectant as well. Although soft and easily cleavable, fluorite is sometimes used as a gemstone—usually cut as a cabochon or relief carving.

SPIRITUAL AND HEALING PROPERTIES

Fluorite helps to assimilate ideas and information from many different sources into conscious awareness. Sudden ideas, inventions, new technologies, and dreams of the future are all encouraged by this stone. Working with the brow chakra, fluorite focuses its energy on the functioning of the mind, helping physical coordination, dexterity, balance, and learning skills. Orderliness and an increased structure in one's affairs are encouraged. Fluorite also helps to maintain the integrity of the skeletal system.

DIVINATORY INTERPRETATION

This crystal works at many different levels, and encourages multilevel activity. In a reading, it indicates that now is the time to make detailed plans. It is essential that circumstances be given some firm shape and direction, or present opportunities may melt away.

Fluorite suggests that you need to sit down and think carefully about what you want and how you can practically achieve your goals. Rather than diving straight into action, sit back and allow new ideas to form. Think about how goals can be acheived and then, in a methodical and organized way, begin to move toward them.

In a negative placement, fluorite suggests cloudy thinking, wasted energy on inappropriate activities, clumsiness, and either too much time daydreaming or not enough time thinking about a specific situation.

SUGGESTED READINGS

Fluorite in center/First House
Remain clearheaded and cautious.

Fluorite in southeast/Second House
Be completely practical in approaching problem-solving.

Fluorite in east/Third House
Don't go ahead with your plans before consulting others about them.

Fluorite in north/Fourth House
You may find yourself forgetting facts and figures unless you get more rest.

Fluorite in west/Fifth House
Walking, swimming, or yoga will help you think more clearly.

Fluorite in Sixth House
Make plans before you rush into any activity associated with work.

Fluorite in southwest/Seventh House
You need to take into account the needs of other people, and to compromise slightly.

Fluorite in Eighth House
The timing of any financial dealings may be crucial.

Fluorite in northeast/Ninth House
All sides of a situation must be seen in order to understand what is going on.

Fluorite in south/Tenth House
Make sure your planning is thorough.

Fluorite in northwest/Eleventh House
You may be asked to plan and organize joint ventures and activities.

Fluorite in Twelfth House
You need some time alone to clarify your plans.

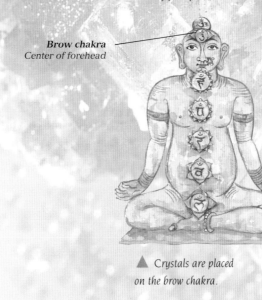

Brow chakra
Center of forehead

▲ *Crystals are placed on the brow chakra.*

▲ ◄ *Most technological advances involve a moment of inspiration followed by painstaking planning. Fluorite can encourage and help organize the inventive mind.*

Personality

Fluorite represents a designer or inventor. These people may seem to be ahead of their time, and typically offer innovative suggestions regarding ways to increase efficiency.

Energy

Inventive, coordinated, integrated.

Sugilite

First identified in Japan in 1944, sugilite is named after its discoverer, Kenichi Sugi.

Sugilite

Color: purple, pink, lilac

Hardness: 5.5–6.5

Composition: KNa_2 $(Fe^2 + Mn^2 + Al)_2 Li_3Si_{12}O_{30}$

Qualities: integrating, balancing

Main chakra: crown

▲▶ *There is often a discrepancy between the lives we lead and the dreams we hold dear. Sugilite can help reintegrate our spiritual integrity into our everyday lives.*

Sugilite forms deep under the ground within volcanic rock. It is part of a group of closely related minerals named osumilites, from the Osumi region of Japan. All osumilites are complex silicates of potassium, sodium, iron, magnesium, and aluminum, and all are very similar in appearance.

Sugilite was not confirmed as a distinct mineral until 1976. It forms as aggregates of small hexagonal crystals, or as massive microcrystalline blocks. The best gem-quality sugilite comes from India and especially South Africa, where it is called royal azel, lavulite, or royal lavulite.

MYTH AND HISTORY

Over two hundred new minerals are identified each year, but few become popular with jewelers or healers. Because of its ability to be easily worked and polished, sugilite is a favorite of jewelers, who cut it into beads and cabochons. Its deep, rich color-ing has also made it popular with healers, who believe that it can help integrate spiritual qualities into the modern age.

SPIRITUAL AND HEALING PROPERTIES

Sugilite works very well at the crown chakra, which acts as a channel for the entrance of universal energies into the body and mind and defines, sustains, and energizes the whole chakra system. Sugilite helps the crown to integrate this influx of spiritual energy into daily living. It can be useful for those who are very sensitive, or who find it difficult to feel at ease with modern life.

Sugilite also strengthens all functions of the nervous system. It is particularly helpful where there is a lack of coordination between the left and right hemispheres of the brain, affecting physical coordination.

DIVINATORY INTERPRETATION

In the areas in which it falls, sugilite suggests the need for a greater integration between spiritual and physical qualities. It may be that the questioner's ideals are too rarefied, and that too much is expected from the effort that is being made. On the other hand, the situation may be suffering because spiritual aspects are being ignored in favor of obvious material benefits. If the stone appears in an area relating to health, it may suggest the need to watch out for clumsiness or a lack of dexterity, as this may be the cause of future problems.

Sugilite may also suggest a sense of alienation within one's surroundings, or of being out of step or perhaps out of one's depth. This will likely be an emotional or personal belief rather than a true evaluation of the situation. Look for common themes and shared aspirations instead of differences in approach and apparent faults.

SUGGESTED READINGS

Sugilite in center/First House
You may feel a need to be seen living your beliefs instead of toeing the line.

Sugilite in southeast/Second House
Isolating yourself from group activities is not the best action at the moment.

Sugilite in east/Third House
Discussions and debates with friends could be helpful for you at present.

Sugilite in north/Fourth House
You may feel out of step from the rest of your family at the moment.

Sugilite in west/Fifth House
Take time to create an original and useful object.

Sugilite in Sixth House
Both your health and your work may be suffering because of internal tensions concerning a conflict of material and spiritual goals in your life.

Sugilite in southwest/Seventh House
Disagreements can be resolved by looking for common ground.

Sugilite in Eighth House
Avoid schemes that seem to be offering something for nothing.

*Crown chakra
Top of the head*

Sugilite in northeast/Ninth House
Opportunities need to be looked at realistically.

Sugilite in south/Tenth House
Your plans should take into account your ideals as well as practical possibilities.

Sugilite in northwest/Eleventh House
A group you are involved with needs to improve its focus in order to succeed.

Sugilite in Twelfth House
Helping others is a useful way to expand your experience.

▲ *Crystals are placed on the crown chakra.*

▲◄ *Practical coordination and an appreciation of harmony in life, especially when working with like-minded groups, helps to maintain the energy of the crown chakra.*

◄ *Sugilite helps preserve the energy balance between the left and right hemispheres of the brain, insuring confidence and clarity, as well as dexterity and physical alertness.*

Personality

Sugilite represents a sensitive person with a lively imagination, but this person likely finds it difficult to socialize with others on an everyday basis.

Energy

Integrated, balanced, alienated.

Amethyst

One of the most popular semiprecious stones, amethyst is produced in a variety of transparent purple shades.

Amethyst

Color: pale violet to deep purple

Hardness: 7

Composition: SiO_2 (quartz)

Qualities: clarifying, calming, integrating

Main chakras: brow, crown

Amethyst is a common variety of quartz. It grows in geodes—crystal-filled spherical cavities that are found within volcanic rock. Despite its popularity, amethyst is classed as semiprecious because of the rarity of gem-quality stones. Amethyst tends to have color zones throughout each crystal rather than consistent shading. Careful heating can disperse the color more evenly, but too much heat will turn the stone to yellow, brown, or green. Some amethysts will fade in daylight very quickly. The cause of the stone's coloration is not known for certain, but one possibility may be a combination of iron atoms in the lattice and radioactive decay.

MYTH AND HISTORY

Amethyst has adorned jewelry for at least 5,000 years. It was cut for seals and rings by the ancient Egyptians, and was popular in both classical Greece and Rome.

There was a common belief that amethyst could prevent the worst effects of too much alcohol, and thus derived its name from the Greek word *amethystos*, meaning "not drunken." A classical tale relates that Bacchus, god of wine and ecstasy, accidentally cursed a young maiden, Amethistos, who was on her way to Diana's temple. About to be torn to pieces by wild animals, she prayed to Diana (moon goddess of chastity and the hunt), who turned her into white stone. Bacchus, acknowledging his error, poured wine over the transformed girl, turning the stone to amethyst.

▶ *The ancient Greek god Bacchus symbolized the unruly and unpredictable energies that amethyst is thought to moderate.*

During the Middle Ages, amethyst was generally associated with an upright and sober mentality. It was thought to calm the passions, increase shrewdness and intelligence, and provide protection from enemies, wild animals, and disease.

SPIRITUAL AND HEALING PROPERTIES

Amethyst is primarily a stone of the mind. It helps to bring calmness and clarity where there is anxiety and confusion. It also integrates and balances all systems of the body, and is thus an important universal healing stone. Amethyst can be a useful stone for meditation and other spiritual exercises, as it calms both the mind and the emotions while keeping awareness sharp and focused. Intuition is also enhanced.

DIVINATORY INTERPRETATION

Amethyst appearing in a reading suggests that there is a need for calm, sober deliberation if decisions are to be made. If the stone falls within areas pertaining to health, there may be issues concerning anxiety, nervous headaches, digestive disorders (often linked to levels of mental stress), or physical coordination problems.

Amethyst in a reading can also be seen as a warning that a degree of self-discipline is needed; now is not the time to have a wild night out on the town. Begin to put things in order, make sense of your priorities, and make sure you are not overdoing anything in your life. Insure that you have your feet on the ground and are not getting carried away by unrealistic, grandiose schemes. Imagination is very important, but it must be focused on practical goals.

SUGGESTED READINGS

Amethyst in center/First House
You have a need to appear to others as calm and in control.

Amethyst in southeast/Second House
Tension could build up and create headaches or stomach upsets. Learn to relax.

Amethyst in east/Third House
Be calm and reasonable in your communications.

Amethyst in north/Fourth House
Keep the balance between your work and home life. Don't let either one dominate.

Amethyst in west/Fifth House
Curb any impulse to take risks or to gamble with money or emotions.

Amethyst in Sixth House
Look after your health as a priority now.

Amethyst in southwest/Seventh House
It is time to make peace with anyone who seems antagonistic toward you.

Amethyst in Eighth House
First impressions can be misleading, so be cautious in making any commitments.

Amethyst in northeast/Ninth House
Avoid being overly enthusiastic in any current plans.

Amethyst in south/Tenth House
Figure out what your priorities are and stick with them.

Amethyst in northwest/Eleventh House
Peaceful and relaxing activities will be helpful at this time.

Amethyst in Twelfth House
You may be experiencing sleep difficulties, restlessness, and anxiety at the moment. Try your hardest to relax.

Crown chakra
Top of the head
Brow chakra
Center of forehead

▲▶ Amethyst was a fashionable gemstone for Victorian jewelry, as it symbolized sobriety, reliability, and spiritual aspiration.

▲ Crystals are placed on the crown and brow chakras.

Personality

An amethyst character will be levelheaded, generous, and fair, and may perhaps be a religious professional of some kind. If this person's spiritual interests have been repressed, however, there may be an excessive use of alcohol or narcotics.

Energy

Self-controlled, calm, considerate.

Milky Quartz

Milky quartz is a cloudy type of rock crystal that contains a myriad of tiny gas or water bubbles.

Milky quartz

Color: opaque white, translucent

Hardness: 7

Composition: SiO_2

Qualities: gentle diffusion, dispersal

Main chakras: sacral, crown

▼ *The presence of quartz-bearing stones in so many megalithic sites throughout the world suggests that the choice of these types of stones was deliberate.*

Many types of rock crystal contain veins and patterns of small bubbles within their clear, transparent interiors, usually caused by water or gas. The base of quartz crystals is often cloudy, with small bubbles; this cloudy section is called milky quartz. Milky quartz can sometimes turn clear when gentle warmth is applied.

MYTH AND HISTORY

Less precious than the transparent variety, milky quartz has not had as exalted a history, but it has been used for making beads for jewelry for some time. It also has a long history of use for demarcating special or sacred spaces. Many megalithic sites in Western Europe have stones with a high milky quartz content. At Newgrange, a megalithic burial site in Ireland built around 3200 BC, the large central ceremonial chamber was given an outer covering of white quartz walls.

SPIRITUAL AND HEALING PROPERTIES

Milky quartz has all the same energies as clear quartz, except that it has a more gentle, feminine effect. Just as it gently diffuses light, so it softly radiates a cool, quiet energy into the aura.

Milky quartz is soothing to both the mind and the emotions. It blends all energies around it together, and has a gentle, purifying effect. It is like rose quartz in many ways, but without the focus on emotional states.

DIVINATORY INTERPRETATION

Milky quartz in a reading indicates that there is some lack of definition or clarity in the situation. This may be causing some frustration, but now is simply not the time to act. Patience is required for the gentle, dissipating effects of milky quartz to bring clarity to the situation.

Keep in mind that a lack of focus may be advantageous in some circumstances—it offers a rest from continuous attention to detail. At any rate, for better or worse, nothing much can be achieved, whether the fogginess is in the mind of the questioner or the surrounding events. It is best to just relax and wait for clarity.

If milky quartz falls in the section that relates to the main thrust of the question, this may suggest that the question itself is lacking in clarity. If this is felt to be the case, rethink your wording or approach and ask the question again.

When milky quartz falls amongst stones of conflict, this suggests that the situation will lose its internal energy naturally, and the negativity will disperse on its own. If found near strong stones, milky quartz will diffuse some of their energy, but it will also help to integrate any conflicting patterns in the way the stones have fallen.

▼ *Short periods of unfocused rest during the day can help to integrate experiences and can lead to problem-solving insights.*

SUGGESTED READINGS

Milky quartz in center/First House
Your question is not clear—try again with a more focused question.

Milky quartz in southeast/Second House
Keep a tight reign on your finances over the next few days.

Milky quartz in east/Third House
You need to be precise when asking others to follow your instructions.

Milky quartz in north/Fourth House
Stay at home, sit quietly, and relax.

Milky quartz in west/Fifth House
Now is not the time to focus on any one project.

Milky quartz in Sixth House
This is not a good time for decisions—wait until the picture is clearer.

Milky quartz in southwest/Seventh House
Relationships may seem insubstantial and unstable at present.

Milky quartz in Eighth House
The timing of events is likely to be erratic or vague, so don't rely too heavily on a rigid schedule.

Milky quartz in northeast/Ninth House
Share your ideas and skills as much as possible.

Milky quartz in south/Tenth House
Your current plans may become irrelevant as the situation develops.

Milky quartz in northwest/Eleventh House
People around you may be confused or annoyed by your lack of clarity.

Milky quartz in Twelfth House
You should not trust your feelings about people or events at the moment.

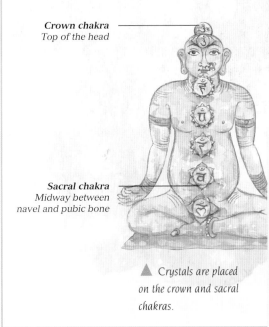

Crown chakra
Top of the head

Sacral chakra
Midway between navel and pubic bone

▲ *Crystals are placed on the crown and sacral chakras.*

Personality

Milky quartz characterizes a rather vague, unfocused individual; he or she is well-meaning, but is not particularly effective in everyday life.

Energy

Vague, confused.

Moonstone

Moonstone has a soft blue-white sheen that is reminiscent of the gentle light cast by the moon.

Moonstone

Color: pearly white, yellow, blue

Hardness: 6–6.5

Composition: $KAlSi_3O_8$ (potassium aluminum silicate)

Qualities: emotionally balancing, intuitive, calming

Main chakras: solar plexus, sacral

▶▶ *Just as the tides rise and fall in response to the gravitational pull of the moon, so moonstone can harmonize the rise and fall of our emotions, helping us to get in touch with our true feelings and to increase our sensitivity toward others.*

Moonstone is the generic name given to a number of related minerals with similar appearances. All moonstones belong to the oligoclase family of feldspars, and are the purest members of this mineral family originating from hot solutions.

Feldspar is one of the most common minerals on the planet. Often displaying interesting plays of light within the crystal structure, it is composed of parallel layers of mineral that reflect the light entering the crystal. Moonstone is unique in its soft iridescence.

MYTH AND HISTORY

Fine crystals of nearly transparent moonstone are commonly found throughout the Mont Blanc mountain range. In fact, another name for moonstone is *adularia*; this name is derived from Mount Adula, near St. Gotthard, in Switzerland, where moonstone is often found. However, it is in India that moonstone has had the longest history. Indian women in particular have long held the stone in high esteem. Not only is it thought to emphasize female virtues, but it is also believed to help alleviate assorted digestive problems, as well as reproductive ailments afflicting women in particular.

SPIRITUAL AND HEALING PROPERTIES

Moonstone is one of the best stones for bringing emotional calm and stability, as it has the ability to quickly release tensions created by emotional stress. This stress often affects the stomach and digestive system, disrupting normal processes of absorbing nutrition from food. Stomachaches and headaches can also be relieved if their source is emotional.

Just as the moon itself has a relationship with water, moods, cycles, and intuition, so does moonstone encourage a fluidity and flexibility in all body systems. Fluid balance can be restored, as can body cycles that have been disrupted through shock and stress. All problems involving the flow of energy, particularly in the female reproductive system, can be eased. Intuition, creativity, and empathy can also increase with moonstone.

DIVINATORY INTERPRETATION

Moonstone has a very feminine energy, and thus, in a reading, it can represent an important female in the questioner's life. It can also stand for the feminine qualities of empathy, listening, and sensitivity.

This stone shows that emotional balance is needed in a situation. Stress may be building up, creating a rigidity in relationships that needs to be loosened. When moonstone falls in an area relating to health, it signals that emotional stress may be creating stomachaches, digestive problems, or headaches.

Moonstone also indicates a need for intuitive skills. Now is not the time for strident action—observe, feel, and sense what is going on within you and around you before you do anything. There are delicate creative energies coming together at this time, and so it is best to proceed with patience and care.

Because the moon controls so many of the life cycles on our planet, moonstone in a reading may indicate that the questioner should be aware that there is a natural cycle of growth to all things. There is no point in trying to rush things—everything happens in its own time.

SUGGESTED READINGS

Moonstone in center/First House
You need to be more approachable and receptive.

Moonstone in southeast/Second House
Learn to trust your gut feelings and stick by them.

Moonstone in east/Third House
You are very intuitive, but you should keep your observations to yourself.

Moonstone in north/Fourth House
There are emotional undercurrents in your family. Tread carefully.

Moonstone in west/Fifth House
Time spent by the sea or near a river will help settle your emotions.

Moonstone in Sixth House
Health problems are likely affecting your digestion.

Moonstone in southwest/Seventh House
Relationships are being clouded by emotions at this time.

Moonstone in Eighth House
Beginnings and endings are a natural part of life. Learn to accept this reality.

Moonstone in northeast/Ninth House
Allow time to absorb new information before acting on it or passing it on to others.

Moonstone in south/Tenth House
Do not rush into anything at this time. Wait at least three days before taking action.

Moonstone in northwest/Eleventh House
Listen to what your friends and acquaintances say before acting.

Moonstone in Twelfth House
You may find yourself easily swayed by other people's strong opinions or feelings.

Solar plexus chakra Midway between navel and base of ribs

Sacral chakra Midway between navel and pubic bone

▲ Crystals are placed on the solar plexus and sacral chakras.

Personality

Moonstone suggests a personality with strong feminine qualities, though not necessarily a woman.

Energy

Emotionally balanced, intuitive, cyclical.

Pearl/ Abalone

Both pearl and abalone shell are organic gemstones derived from shellfish.

Pearl

Color: white, pink, brown, black

Hardness: 2.5–3.5

Composition: $CaCO_3$ + conchiolin + H_2O

Qualities: tolerant, flexibile

Main chakra: sacral

Abalone

Color: iridescent blues, greens, silver, red

Hardness: 3.5–4

Composition: variable $CaCO_3$

Qualities: flexible, immune

Main chakras: heart, sacral

Pearl and abalone shell are variable compounds, but are both basically comprised of the same mineral: calcium carbonate. (The gemstones aragonite and calcite are also made of this compound in inorganic form.)

Pearls form inside the shells of certain mollusks in both the sea and in fresh water as a response to the irritation of grains of sand or parasites. Their iridescence is caused by light dispersing from the microcrystals of calcium carbonate. Abalone is a widespread, edible shellfish that has an inner shell with many shiny, iridescent colors, mainly blues and greens.

MYTH AND HISTORY

The name "pearl" is thought to derive from the Latin word *pernula*, the diminuitive of the word *perna*, meaning "sea shell" or "mussel."

Pearl is a very soft gemstone with little resistance to impact, chemicals, or drying conditions, but it has always been regarded as one of the most precious of jewels for its rarity and beauty. Traditionally, perfectly clear, unblemished, round pearls were the primary gemstone of the moon in India. When set in silver, they were thought to have the power to remove problems caused by an inauspicious placement of the moon in one's natal chart. In both India and China, the pearl is the epitome and symbol of purity, excellence, longevity, immortality, enlightenment, and wisdom.

Abalone shell is much more robust than pearl, and has been used in many cultures as a decoration for inlays into carvings and for jewelry. A disc of abalone shell is worn on the forehead of Apache girls as they greet the sun on the morning of their initiation into womanhood.

Mother-of-pearl is made of essentially the same material as abalone shell and pearl. It is the thick layer on the inner surface of shells from which pearls are grown—hence its common name. It is also known as "nacre."

▲ ◄ *A pearl choker from the early 1900's.*
► *Pearls with a perfect luster and shape are rare, making the best specimens very costly.*

SPIRITUAL AND HEALING PROPERTIES

Pearl is thought to be the finest stabilizer of the emotions. It increases tolerance and flexibility, and brings relaxation where there has been tension and frustration. Digestive functions are eased, and there is an increase in self-assuredness. All functions of a watery nature or involving a flow of some sort within the body are regulated by pearl.

Abalone strengthens the structure of the body and the functions of the heart chakra. Increased emotional expression and a strengthening of the immune system can also be expected. As well, abalone encourages individuality and expansion.

DIVINATORY INTERPRETATION

Both pearl and abalone shell have the same divinatory meanings: they are intimately connected to the sea, and to the tides of the emotions. An easy flow of feelings, sensitivity to others, and awareness of personal needs are all indicated in a positive, balanced reading.

Very often, these gems will represent the family, particularly the mother. Their highly changeable coloration suggests that, like our human emotions, matters are in a state of continual flux. In these situations, there is no point in expecting matters to settle down. Life is all about change, and these gems remind us that nothing stays the same for long—especially where the emotions are concerned. Like the play of colors in pearl and abalone, change is the beauty of existence.

In places where these gems appear, you may need to allow matters to flow more

SUGGESTED READINGS

Pearl/abalone in center/First House
You need to place family concerns first on your priority list.

Pearl/abalone in southeast/Second House
Don't rely on resources that you don't actually possess or own.

Pearl/abalone in east/Third House
Try to be sensitive and delicate in your communications.

Pearl/abalone in north/Fourth House
Look to the women in your family for guidance and support.

Pearl/abalone in west/Fifth House
Appreciate the beauty of the situation and try to adjust to whatever is happening.

Pearl/abalone in Sixth House
Be flexible to events at work and tune in to underlying emotions.

Pearl/abalone in southwest/Seventh House
Try to be sensitive and patient with the moods of those around you.

Pearl/abalone in Eighth House
Family or relationship issues from the past may resurface.

Pearl/abalone in northeast/Ninth House
Don't commit yourself to any specific viewpoint or stance—keep an open mind.

Pearl/abalone in south/Tenth House
No single path to the future can be guaranteed given the present fluctuation in events.

Pearl/abalone in northwest/Eleventh House
Friends may need consoling or nurturing, and may look to you to provide these comforts.

Pearl/abalone in Twelfth House
Spend some time by the sea or watching the cycle of the moon in order to reconnect to nature's energies.

Heart chakra
Center of breastbone in center of chest

Sacral chakra
Midway between navel and pubic bone

▲ *Crystals are placed on the heart and sacral chakras.*

easily. Frustration and annoyance can be countered by directing your attention elsewhere, to where harmony and relaxation reside. In a positive position, these gems can show harmony in relationships; in a difficult cast, they may show areas of friction.

 Pearls have long been linked with mourning, and were typically used to adorn memorial brooches.

Personality

Pearl and abalone personalities may be outwardly beautiful and inwardly confused. A great deal of emotional energy exists. However, if there is no balancing factor, this may lead to instability.

Energy

Sensitive, family-oriented, confused.

Peacock ore

A familiar mineral, peacock ore is best known for its bright surface colors of yellow, mauve, blue, and red.

Peacock ore

Color: brassy yellow with bright blue, red, mauve

Hardness: 3–4

Composition: CuFeS$_4$ (chalcopyrite, sulfide of copper and iron)

Qualities: synthesizing, clearing

Main chakra: solar plexus

▶ *The name "peacock ore" is an old miner's term, yet it is undeniably an apt description of this stone, given that its intense iridescent colors do indeed resemble the plumage of a peacock.*

▶▶ *As a tool for healing, peacock ore can be used to lower calcium levels in the body, which can be helpful in treating arthritic conditions.*

Peacock ore is the common name for two related minerals, bornite and chalcopyrite. Both minerals are sulfides of iron and copper, and both commonly occur in copper-ore-bearing rocks. Chalcopyrite is a bright, brassy yellow color, while bornite's coloration is more reddish brown. After the surface of either mineral has been exposed to some degree of weathering, a tarnish forms. This tarnish is comprised of assorted copper oxides or hydroxides, which form a thin layer over the mineral. When light strikes the tarnished surface, the result is a refraction into iridescent rainbow colors, similar to the effect of oil on water.

MYTH AND HISTORY

There is no doubt that peacock ore, as a primary ore of copper, has been known of since ancient times. Today, chalcopyrite is a primary industrial source of copper due to the fact that it is found in large quantities around the world; notable sources include Chile, Peru, Bolivia, Mexico, and the USA.

SPIRITUAL AND HEALING PROPERTIES.

With its wide range of colors, peacock ore has the ability to stimulate each of the main chakras, as well as all of the subtle energy systems of the body. This process is helped along by the mineral's high copper content, which allows for a greater flow and integration of energy patterns.

Integration is one of the primary functions of this stone. The underlying golden color relates directly to the solar plexus chakra, and thus peacock ore naturally encourages happiness and self-empowerment. It also provides protection from negativity. The presence of iron, copper, and sulfur hints at a strengthening of the circulatory and nervous systems, along with the physical structures of the body.

DIVINATORY INTERPRETATION

Peacock ore can improve the general outlook within any area in a reading because it has the power to bring all possibilities to bear. Just as peacock ore's wide variety of colors derives from the underlying gold-colored rock, so a situation characterized by an underlying sense of contentment can lead to a variety of desirable outcomes.

Confidence is one of the main messages of this stone. Its appearance in a reading implies that success will be achieved in time, no matter what critics say. At this time, you should be able to integrate all aspects of the situation in a productive way.

Even in a difficult placement, peacock ore suggests that opportunities exist for happiness, as every experience, whether good or bad, creates new possibilities.

SUGGESTED READINGS

Peacock ore in center/First House
An air of confidence will help to create an impression that others will trust.

Peacock ore in southeast/Second House
Find ways of being content with your financial and personal resources.

Peacock ore in east/Third House
When offering advice, make sure you are positive and supportive.

Peacock ore in north/Fourth House
Spend some time at home cleaning, tidying, and reorganizing in order to secure a base for yourself.

Peacock ore in west/Fifth House
Allow yourself to experience the joy of natural surroundings.

Peacock ore in Sixth House
Developing a positive outlook will help you to release the stress that has been building up.

Peacock ore in southwest/Seventh House
Start appreciating the value of your relationships and partnerships.

Peacock ore in Eighth House
Take time to pull together your diverse skills and focus them on a goal.

Peacock ore in northeast/Ninth House
Be open to whatever the universe offers you.

Peacock ore in south/Tenth House
Success is here, though you may not realize or appreciate it fully.

Peacock ore in northwest/Eleventh House
Spend time with those who share your views and philosophies on life.

Peacock ore in Twelfth House
Take time out to contemplate your potential and possibilities for growth.

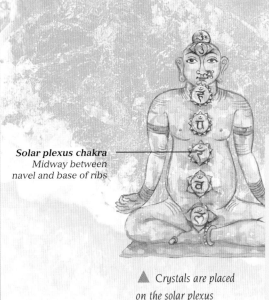

Solar plexus chakra
Midway between navel and base of ribs

▲ *Crystals are placed on the solar plexus chakra.*

Personality

Peacock ore is characterized by a mature and widely experienced person. This person is also enthusiastic, with an underlying confidence in life.

Energy

Joyful, integrated.

Crystal Magic

Magic is often the next natural step following divination. Whereas divination clarifies the nature of the energies within the situation at hand and can indicate a likely outcome, magic enables the diviner to work with this information to encourage a favorable outcome. With divination, we diagnose; with magic, we offer the appropriate medicine. Indeed, like medicine, magic is a powerful tool. And like the wrong medicine, the wrong magic can do more harm than good.

Magicians of the past saw the universe as a giant web of interconnected energies. They learned which threads needed to be moved in order to accomplish the change that they desired. They also discovered that when one thread is removed the whole web changes. This wisdom has permeated our consciousness today, and we understand that it is never possible to act without consequences. Similarly, in the realm of magic, it is important to understand that there may be consequences to the magic you do, and that you are wholly responsible for your actions.

Magic is a way of focusing your mind, will, emotions, and actions to affect an outcome. The only difference between an ordinary act and a magical act is that magic does not work with things, but rather with symbols and rituals. We use muscles to change things in the ordinary way, whereas we use the mind to change things in the magical way.

On the following pages are three magical spells involving crystals that can help you improve certain areas of your life.

Invisibility and Protection from Harm

This spell can protect you from those people and things that might bear you malice. It should be used only in situations where invisibility will be beneficial, and not in cases where it would be harmful—when crossing the road for example!

You will need:
- A transparent, clear crystal such as quartz, calcite, or fluorite
- One red stone, one blue stone, one green stone, and one yellow stone
- A bowl or jar of water (a vessel with a dark interior will work best)

Place the bowl of water on a table. Pick up the red stone (representing the element of fire) and say:

Stone of fire
to ashes turn all
harm that hunts me.

Repeat this verse several times while holding the stone to your solar plexus, which is your own fire energy center.

Put the stone down beside the bowl and say:

Hide me from hurt.

Next, pick up the blue stone (representing the element of water) and say:

Stone of water
melt, dissolve, disperse
all ill that stalks me.

Repeat this verse several times while holding the stone below your navel, which is your own water center.

Lay the stone at the opposite side of the bowl to the fire stone and say:

Hide me from hurt.

Now pick up the green stone (representing the element of air) and say:

Stone of air
scatter like leaves
ill thoughts and intentions.

Repeat this verse several times while holding the stone to the heart center in the middle of the chest.

Lay the stone to the left of the fire stone by the bowl and say:

Hide me from hurt.

Pick up the yellow stone (representing the element of earth) and say:

Stone of earth
hold fast and hide
No foes will find me..

Repeat this verse several times while holding the stone at the base of your spine.

Place the stone by the bowl opposite the green stone and say:

Hide me from hurt.

Now, take the clear crystal in your hands and say:

As fire I cannot be held
As air I cannot be seen
As water I flow around all obstacles
As earth I am unshakable

Look at the clear stone in your hands. Repeat the words "as clear as crystal" many times, all the while imagining that your whole being, from the inside out, has taken on the same transparency and brilliance as the stone. When this image is clear in your mind, carefully place the stone in the bowl. Watch as its edges become indistinct and difficult to see. To remind yourself of the state you wish to stay in, occasionally repeat the words "as clear as crystal," and remember the crystal disappearing as it entered the water. To end the spell, thank each element in turn and dismantle the arrangement of stones.

◀ ◀ *It is important to take time to really feel the power of the spell as it builds up. The more involved you become, the more effective the outcome will be.*

Spell for Abundance and the Fulfillment of Wishes

Although it often seems to be linked to external factors, abundance is created internally and at subtle levels of thought and feeling. Dissatisfaction, emptiness, and a sense of poverty are indications that we have become separated and isolated from the beneficial energies of the universe. This spell is for increasing abundance in one's life. It focuses on re-establishing strong links that will allow opportunities and desires to be recognized and fulfilled.

You will need:
● One red stone
● A few yellow stones
● A few green stones

First, cleanse the stones you are going to use (see page 28). Begin the spell by sitting quietly and thinking clearly about the reasons why you wish to work the spell. Close your eyes and imagine red roots extending down from where you are in contact with the ground. Feel those energies diving deep toward the center of the Earth. Send your breath down these roots and feel solid and well rooted.

Now say the words "I am supported." Take the red stone and place it centrally within the space where you are performing the spell. Again, say the words "I am supported."

Close your eyes once again. Visualize golden rays, beams, or threads shooting out from your solar plexus. See them streaming away from you in all directions, contacting everything around, above, and below you. Feel yourself at the center of a web of golden light. When the image is strong, say "I am nourished."

Take the yellow stones and arrange them concentrically around the red stone. When all the stones are placed, say once again "I am nourished."

Now close your eyes once more. From the area of light at your solar plexus, imagine a seedling sprouting up toward your heart. As it reaches your heart it forms a large green flower bud. As you watch, the bud slowly opens its beautiful

▲ *Choose stones that you find particularly attractive for your spells. Buying stones for a special purpose will infuse them with the energy of your intention.*

green petals. Green light fills the whole of your body and gently radiates into the space around you. Say, "I am abundant. The wishes in my heart are instantly fulfilled." As you say this, the final petals open up to reveal a brilliant green gemstone or crystal in the heart of the flower. If you have a particular wish, focus your attention on the jewel and think about it.

When you are ready, open your eyes and place the green stones in a concentric circle around the other stones. Again, say "I am abundant. The wishes in my heart are instantly fulfilled."

Sit and look at the stones for a little while. You can now either leave them in place, or clap your hands and clear the stones away. Remembering the jewel within the flower during the day will maintain your energy link.

▲◄ *Although the power of spells comes from the focus of the mind, intense concentration is not necessary, especially when the outcome is strongly desired.*
◄ *Visualization does not need microscopic clarity to be effective. Feel the power of the words and let the pictures develop in their own way, at their own speed. Practice will eventually bring clear imagery.*

Healing Spell

All illness, whether it be physical, emotional, or mental, arises from the wrong sort of energy being in the wrong place at the wrong time. Problems begin when the individual is unable to rebalance his or her energy equilibrium. This spell is designed to lift out excess energy and to return it to a place where it can be used in a life-giving way. Remember that, whatever anyone else may do or wish to do, the healing ultimately comes from the ill person themselves—only the body can repair itself. Sometimes, for various reasons, a person holds onto a diseased state, or continually invites repeating patterns of illness. Only an internal change of heart and mind will end this cycle.

Though you may be successful in removing the subtle levels of imbalance, it is important to realize that the physical body can still take a long time to heal itself. It should also be acknowledged that positive thoughts can be as powerful as anything else. Lastly, remember that it is unwise to become overly attached to outcomes and results. Do your work, and then let the universe do its work.

If you are using the healing spell on someone else, make sure that you have their permission before you start.

You will need:
- A small mirror or a piece of paper with a body outline drawn onto it
- The name or signature and a piece of hair or other item belonging to the person you wish to heal
- A selection of crystals
- A candle
- Incense
- A bowl of water
- A handful of pure rock salt or sea salt

First, create a space that represents the person you wish to help. If you have a small mirror, use this to represent the person. Alternatively, on a good-sized piece of paper, draw a rough outline of a figure or a simple elongated oval shape. This drawing will represent the person—both his or her physical form and his or her surrounding auric field.

If you have some hair, or a signature or photograph belonging to the person to be healed, place it on your representation and write the person's name underneath it. Take a minute to look at the representation and think about the person and his or her situation.

Next, carefully lay out your crystals and say:

> You stones that are the bones
> of all things
> in all places
> through all time;
> you stones that help
> and heal
> come here to me;
> you healing spirits
> listen to my heart,
> show me those that
> can help [name of person].

Close your eyes for a moment. When you feel ready, open them and gaze at your stones. Some stones will immediately draw your attention. Pick four of them out and set them aside. Thank the remaining stones and then clear them away.

Sitting down, imagine yourself completely surrounded by an electric-blue aura, especially your hands and fingers. Take each selected stone and, with awareness, slowly pass it over the person's representation, visualizing at the same time imbalances and illness being drawn into the crystal. If you wish to use words here to help you, just say whatever comes to mind.

You may find that certain areas of the representation feel different. Spend more time holding the stone over these areas, letting your intuition guide you. After you have swept over the entire representation, the imbalances within the stone will need to be returned to their proper place in the universe. There are four ways to do this: through fire, air, water, and earth. All four ways are effective for all stones; the choice of which to use for each stone is up to you.

Through fire: Pass the stone above a candle flame and say:

> Spirit of Fire
> Spirit of Flame
> Restore all to light
> Restore all to balance

Through water: Sweep the stone through the bowl of water and say:

> Spirit of Water
> Ocean of cleansing
> Wash away all debris
> Wash away all dust

Through air: Pass the crystal through incense smoke and say:

> Spirit of Air
> Breath of life
> Bring purity
> Bring joy

Through earth: Cover the stone with dry sea or rock salt and say:

> Spirit of Earth
> Ground of bearing
> Return to strength
> Return to contentment

After having gone through a cleansing, each stone will be free of any imbalances picked up during the healing process. Where the person is extremely unwell, you can perform the spell four times with each stone, cleansing the stones after each turn.

Throw away the salt and water and extinguish the candle and incense, thanking each element in turn for its help. Wash the stones in cool water. Visualize the blue aura around you and see it expand outward and disperse. Repeat this spell every few days, if necessary.

◄ ◄ *Collect all of the necessary ingredients for the spell together and arrange them in a satisfying way, so that they are within easy reach.*

◄ *Although you may be concerned about the health of the person on whose behalf you are performing the spell, it is important that your mind be quiet and that you feel confident that whatever you achieve will be useful.*

Index

Resource Directory

USA

Crystal Magic
2978 West Hwy. 89A
Sedona, AZ 86336
Tel (520) 282-1622
Fax (520) 282-1147

Great South Gems and Minerals
38 Bond Drive
Ellenwood, GA 30294
Toll-free (888) 933-4367
Fax (770) 474-4507
Web www.greatsouth.net

Multistone International
135 South Holliday St.
Strasburg, VA 22657
Tel (540) 465-8777
Fax (540) 465-8773
Web www.multistoneintl.com

Pisces Trading
Tel (800) 859-4001
Outside US (503) 287-6258
Fax (800) 859-4001
Web www.bestcrystals.com

Quantum Alchemy
1209 East 9th Avenue
Denver, CO 80218
Toll free (800) 863-0548
Web www.quantumalchemy.com

Rosley's Rocks and Gems
2153 N. Sheffield Ave.
Chicago, IL 60614
Toll free (800) 844-1498
Fax (773) 868-4383
Web www.crystalmaster.com

UK

Charlie's Rock Shop
Unit 14, 1929 Shop
18 Watermill Way
Merton Abbey Mills
London SW19 2RD
Tel (020) 8544-1207

Crystal Classics
The Old Linbay
Woodcockhayes Farm
Willand, Devon EX15 2QF
Tel (0188) 482-1563

Opie Gems
Glyn-Car, Paradise Valley
Llangynin, St Clears
Camarthen, Wales SA33 4JY
Tel (0199) 423-0212

Credits

Quarto would like to thank and acknowledge the following for supplying the pictures reproduced in this book:

(Key: l left, r right, c center, t top, b bottom)

p10 Image Bank, l The Art Archive; p16 Whitney Abrams; p17t The Art Archive b Trip/c Gray; p22cr Image Bank; p24 The Art Archive; p25tr J-L Charmet; p31 Image Bank; p32bl Pictor; p34bl The Art Archive; p47 Image Bank; p56 The Art Archive; p69 Pictor; p70br The Art Archive; p72 The Art Archive; p75 The Art Archive; p78 Pictor; p85 The Art Archive; p90 The Art Archive; p91 The Art Archive; p94 The Art Archive; p95b The Art Archive; p99b The Art Archive; p100 Pictor; p106bl The Art Archive; p107c The Art Archive; p108bl Pictor International, br The Art Archive; p110b The Art Archive; p111b The Art Archive; p112b The Art Archive; p113b The Art Archive; p114b Ruta Brown; p117bl Pictor; p124c Pictor International; p125t The Art Archive; p126b The Art Archive; p128b Image Bank; p129b Pictor; The Art Archive; p99 The Art Archive; p117 Pictor

All other photographs and illustrations are the copyright of Quarto Publishing plc.

While every effort has been made to credit contributors, Quarto would like to apologize should there have been any omissions or errors.

Quarto would like to thank the staff of Charlie's Rock Shop, particularly Charlie, for kindly loaning us their beautiful crystals for photography.

The author would like to thank Simon Lilly for his contributions, clear thinking, and support.